The white-blouse revolution

The white-blouse revolution

Female office workers since 1870

edited by Gregory Anderson

Manchester University Press
Manchester and New York

Distributed exclusively in the USA and Canada by St. Martin's Press

Copyright © Manchester University Press 1988

Whilst copyright in the volume as a whole is vested in Manchester University Press, copyright in individual chapters belongs to their respective authors, and no chapter may be reproduced wholly or in part without express permission in writing of both author and publisher.

Published by Manchester University Press
Oxford Road, Manchester M13 9PL, UK
and Room 400, 175 Fifth Avenue,
New York, NY 10010, USA

British Library cataloguing in publication data
The White-blouse revolution : female office
   workers since 1870
   1. Great Britain. Women clerical personnel,
   1870–1988
   I. Anderson, Gregory
   331.4'8165137'0941

Library of Congress cataloging in publication data
The White-blouse revolution : female office workers since 1870 /
   edited by Gregory Anderson.
      p. cm.
      Includes index.
      Contents: The white-blouse revolution / Gregory Anderson—Women
   clerical workers in the late nineteenth and early twentieth
   centuries / Jane E. Lewis—Pioneers in a dead-end profession /
   Susanne Dohrn—Commercial education and the female office worker /
   Gladys Carnaffan—Get out and get under / Meta Zimmeck—The
   feminisation of the clerical labour force since the Second World War
   / Rosemary Crompton—Beyond feminisation / Margaret L. Hedstrom.
      ISBN 0-7190-2400-5
      1. Women clerks—History.   I. Anderson, Gregory.
   HD6073.M39W58 1989
   331.4'8165137—dc 19   88-25016

ISBN 0 7190 2400 5 *hardback*

Typeset in Great Britain by
Megaron, Cardiff, Wales
Printed in Great Britain by GD.
Anchor Press Ltd., Tiptree, Essex

Contents

Illustrations

Notes on contributors

Gregory Anderson (editor) is Lecturer in Economic History, University of Salford. Publications include *Victorian Clerks*, 1976 and numerous essays and articles on white-collar work and workers.

Jane Lewis teaches in the Social Science and Administration Department at the London School of Economics. Publications include *The Politics of Motherhood: child and maternal welfare in England, 1900–1939*, 1980, and *Women in England: sexual divisions and social change, 1870–1950*, 1984.

Susanne Dohrn works as a freelance journalist near Hamburg in West Germany. Publications include *Die Entstehung weiblicher Buroarbeit in England, 1840 bis 1914* (The Development of women's clerical work in England, 1840 to 1914), 1986.

Gladys Carnaffan is Senior Lecturer in the Department of Management and Professional Studies, Newcastle upon Tyne Polytechnic.

Meta Zimmeck is currently completing a PhD thesis on the employment of women in the British Civil Service, 1870–1939. She has written articles on the history of income tax, women in clerical work and various aspects of the history of the Civil Service. She works as a tape transcriber for the Royal Courts of Justice.

Rosemary Crompton is Senior Lecturer in the School of Economic and Social Studies, University of East Anglia. Publications include *White-Collar Proletariat: Gender and Deskilling in Clerical Work* (with Gareth Jones), 1984, and *Gender and Stratification* (ed. with Michael Mann), 1986.

Margaret L. Hedstrom is an Archivist at the New York State Archives and Records Administration, Albany, New York. She is presently working on a social history of office automation in the US.

1 Gregory Anderson

The white-blouse revolution

Kingsway Building, Export dept. Sept 29th 1911.

'Ten thousand women marched through the streets of London saying 'We will not be dictated to' and went off to become stenographers' (G. K. Chesterton).

If G. K. Chesterton's wry observation suggests little sympathy for the political and social aspirations of the late Victorian feminists, it brilliantly captures the essential predicament of educated working women at that time – the scarcity of suitable job opportunities. More importantly, when set against long-run economic and social change, it described the beginnings of a revolution in the composition of the labour market which is still working itself out a century later. It is the purpose of this essay to explore the causes, course and effects of this revolution.

The starting point is the increasing specialisation and division of labour which has followed the process of structural change associated with modern economic growth. This is partly mirrored in the long-term changes in the sector shares of employment. The employment effects of structural change have strongly favoured the service sector with a pronounced rise in its share of the labour force since the nineteenth century. Increasingly white-collar workers have come to dominate the occupational structures of modern economies. Radical changes have followed both in the places where people work and the kind of work they do. Offices and office-related work have characterised the increase in white-collar employment. While professional, managerial, technical and sales workers have all increased their share of the labour force, it is clerks, the archetypal office workers, who have been the largest and generally fastest growing category of service employment. The huge increase in the number of clerks has been matched by an equally important shift in the sexual composition of clerical work. No other occupation has changed its sex label so completely and so quickly. Indeed the rising female share of the labour force in Britain and other advanced economies is largely explained by the dramatic increase in the female share of white-collar occupations, especially clerical work, since the proportion of women among manual workers has only fluctuated slightly. Although clerical work is now the largest single occupation available to women and the modern office is mainly staffed by women, the feminisation of clerical work was achieved quite early. Already by 1921, 46 per cent of Britain's clerks were women and this process had already occurred in the United States where 52·5 per cent of clerks were women by 1930.[1]

Women began to be recruited into office work in significant numbers from the 1880s with the rate of increase accelerating in the decade or so before the First World War. These first women clerks were truly pioneers because they were entering an almost exclusively male-dominated labour market. When A. V. Munby encountered female 'city' clerks in the London of the 1860s they evoked considerable curiosity in him.[2] This was hardly surprising since in 1851 a mere nineteen women were listed as commercial clerks in England and Wales. In the middle decades of the nineteenth century there were few signs of the imminent transformation of the office workforce. Clerks were men, employed in relatively small but strategically important numbers in the counting-houses of merchants and manufacturers as well as in the growing departments of central and local government. Most of the clerks were employed in small workforces, on average no more than four including office lads and apprentices. Many employers carried out their business with the aid of one full-time clerk. Although the spectrum of male clerkdom was very wide and hard-pressed Cratchit-like figures in dead-end jobs certainly existed, most clerks were superior in social background and educational attainment to other workers. They possessed higher levels of literacy and numeracy while their personal qualities of loyalty, courtesy, honesty and sobriety – in a word respectability – were regarded highly by their employers. The technical and organisational realities of the early offices ensured that such men filled positions of trust and could anticipate long careers ending in management. Given the low level of office technology, the clerks' individual skills were often well developed and highly skilled. Hand-written correspondence between firms was an important aspect of office work and those clerks who could compose business letters well were among the most useful to an employer. The relatively high earnings of good correspondence clerks in the pre-mechanised office suggests that quasi-rents were being earned at that time. Organisationally, the borderline between clerical and managerial functions was not clearly drawn and office practices were often particular to individual firms. This led to increased opportunities for upward mobility. Clerks, in any case, did not regard themselves either simply or solely as trusted lieutenants to the captains of industry; the more enterprising and ambitious among them expected to join the employer class themselves. To that end clerical work was widely regarded as a necessary apprenticeship before setting up in business. Before the 1880s a relatively small-scale, male-dominated world evolved in clerical work in which male clerks pursued their careers mostly untroubled by serious competition in the labour market or changes in the organisation and technology of office work. From then on, developments began to occur which threatened this equilibrium and ultimately signalled the end of the old counting-house world.[3]

In the last third of the century, a combination of factors created a rising demand for clerical labour. The structure of the late-Victorian economy began to shift towards services, with more white-collar workers needed to run an increasingly urban society and to manage the external foreign trade and financial services sector focused on the City of London. Internally, there was a growing division of labour throughout the non-agricultural sectors of the economy which saw more clerks employed in manufacturing as well as in services. In 1911, 42 per cent of all Britain's commercial clerks were employed in the manufacturing sector, where a larger proportion of the workforce was now involved in the coordination and integration of the production process. The number of firms outside manufacturing involved in transactions between producers and consumers also grew rapidly, especially in areas such as finance and trade, while Government, at central and local levels, increased its role both in the provision of services and as a regulator of private economic and other activities. These economy-wide changes led to a marked increase in the demand for clerks with the numbers rising rapidly between the 1880s and the First World War. Already in 1881 there were 208,116 commercial clerks and 46,257 clerks and officers employed in the Civil Service, but by 1911 these categories had expanded to 546,948 and 108,386 respectively. Moreover these figures exclude the substantial rise in the numbers in insurance, banking and the law.[4]

The Causes of Feminisation

While there was an increased demand for all clerks, women were recruited into office work at a proportionately faster rate than men. From very small beginnings in 1881 women had by 1911 increased their share of the commercial and civil service workforces by up to 25 per cent or more. The absolute rise in their numbers was spectacular, from 7,444 to 146,133 in commerce and from 4,657 to 27,129 in the Civil Service. But the historical statistics do reveal marked variations in the nature and extent of feminisation in these early decades. Female civil servants were concentrated overwhelmingly in the Post Office, where they were employed as office auxiliaries rather than as full-time clerks, initially as telegraphists and later as telephonists. And in the private sector while women made major inroads into the commercial office, they made little headway into the male reserves of banking, railways and the law.

The new opportunities for female clerks coincide with major changes in the size and internal organisation of the office. Although the small counting-house of Victorian commerce persisted well into the twentieth century, offices were getting larger and more complex. This was partly allied to changes in business organisation such as the joint-stock company in Britain and the corporation in the United States, but also to the increase in takeovers and amalgamations and the growth of multi-branch organisations. Specialisation and the internal division of labour inside the office matched similar developments in the wider economy outside. Departmentalisation became a feature of the larger and most advanced offices and there was an enormous proliferation in record keeping and correspondence. Office workers at the turn of the century faced a rising tide of information and documentation. One response of employers to the increasing volume of office work was to simply increase the size of the office workforce. Although more male clerks were recruited, their employment faced firms with a problem, a rising wage bill associated with the career expectations of male clerks. Offices could no longer be run on slender resources as in the past and Boards of Directors exerted pressure to curtail costs.

One example will suffice to show how this process operated. The Liverpool-based Union Marine Insurance Company was a typical medium-sized firm dealing by the 1900s with a growing business and extra workload arising from the takeover of smaller companies and the increase in the volume and complexity of marine insurance business. Insurance was a male-dominated business with some men, such as underwriters, being paid high salaries with regular increases to prevent them being poached by rival companies. At the Union Marine a number of expedients was used to control staffing costs: vacancies sometimes remained unfilled, salary increases were refused except where they were automatic and 'volunteers' (who worked for nothing to gain experience) and temporary clerks were used. Despite the best efforts of the Company Secretary, the Board was unable to prevent the male staff rising from 54 in 1905 to 82 by 1913. One expedient was successful: the recruitment of a small number of women. In 1904 the Secretary reported to the Board that the great mass of correspondence has been steadily on the increase and it may be necessary to increase the staff.[5] No change was made that year but junior male clerks were learning shorthand and typewriting in both the Correspondence and Policy Departments where hand-written policies were being abolished. In 1905 the first lady typists were recruited when the firm moved into its new office and although only seven were in place in 1913 compared to eighty-two men, they released junior male clerks (a scarce resource) for training and deployment elsewhere, thus helping the company to control its costs by internal promotion rather than resort to the external labour market.

Although the increase in staff helped cope with the increased production and transmission of information and documents, offices would have become unmanageable and eventually swamped unless the mechanisation of these processes had occurred. Technical change was the other major link with feminisation. Telegraphy and later telephony were vital in speeding-up the transmission of information and led to the creation of armies of female office auxiliaries, but it was the typewriter which revolutionised the production of documents inside the office. The invention and marketing of a successful typewriter from the 1870s in the United States and the 1880s in Britain (with Remington's in the vanguard) meant that a substitute had at last been found for the laborious, costly and time-consuming writing by hand. The time-saving element was important. Typewriters did not save on labour in any overall sense; rather they helped employers save on transcription time, speed up work processes and meet the rising demand for clerical output by reducing the cost of clerical imput, i.e. by employing large numbers of cheaper but efficient female clerks.

Typewriting was a gender-free skill in the beginning and there was no reason why male clerks could not acquire it for themselves. Indeed, some did and many male clerks were trained in shorthand, before it became intrinsically linked to typewriting. Shorthand, recognised as an important aid in correpondence, had a much longer commercial history than typewriting, dating from Pitman's system in Britain in the 1830s with later modifications carried out by John Gregg in the 1880s. Employers encouraged their clerks to acquire shorthand, given its time-saving qualities, while clerks themselves saw it as an important entry qualification in an increasingly overstocked labour market. Shorthand was no panacea and did not, as some had hoped, professionalise clerical work. Once it became linked with typewriting and quickly feminised, men were discouraged from pursuing it for its own sake because they would be considered too useful as shorthand clerks to be given promotion.[6] While men steered clear of being labelled shorthand typists, fearful of becoming mere letter-writing machines, women flocked into typewriting in such numbers that for a while 'typewriter' was synonymous not simply with the machine but with the female operator. Although typists were not enumerated separately from other clerks in Britain before 1931, it is clear that typewriting was dominated by women and that many female clerks were actually typists. A survey of female clerical wages and conditions carried out in 1905–6 found that among 220 respondents no less than 209 described themselves as shorthand typists.[7] Caradog-Jones, writing between the wars, believed that even when women described themselves as clerks or book-keepers they were in reality clerk-typists.[8] Typing was dominated by women. By 1931 only 5,155 men in England and Wales were enumerated as typists compared to 212,296 women. Further confirmation is available from the United States, where by 1930 over 95 per cent off all typists and stenographers were women.[9]

By the end of the nineteenth century, typewriters were becoming well-established in British offices. Typewriters were relatively cheap but even so many employers in the early days did not purchase them. Intermediaries were quick to emerge in the market-place. Typewriting offices were soon providing firms not only with typewriting facilities but also training women on the spot in the new skills.[10] In London in the 1890s these typewriting offices were run by rival typewriter companies. In addition, some women acquired typewriters themselves and complete with movable capital, hired out their services. Juliet Appleton, the heroine of Olive Rayner's *Typewriter Girl*, acquired her first job because she possessed her own machine.[11] Firms later acquired typewriters for themselves, but they did not invest in the training of female typists. One reason for this reluctance lay in the nature of typing skills. Typists possessed a general skill which could easily be transferred between firms. Employers would be reluctant to invest in the training of workers who could then be 'poached' by competitors. In addition, employers did not anticipate young female clerks staying long in their employment. There was a high turnover of female clerks who, like other female workers, stayed only until marriage at this time.

In fact, there was no pressing need for employers to make such an investment. The creation of potential openings for women in the office coincided with widespread improvements in girls' education. Clerical work (along with school-teaching and nursing) was unusual among female occupations before the First World War in that it required some

educational commitment. Education beyond the elementary level was
necessary. 'It is not advisable for girls', a contemporary Handbook of
Employment warned, 'who have only attended an elementary school
to become typists, as their education is not sufficiently advanced to
render them competent. A girl leaving a secondary school at sixteen
years of age is about the right age for beginning'.[12] The very first
women entering commercial offices in the 1880s were products either
of education at home by governesses or of the expansion of voluntary
secondary education for girls, which occurred after 1850. The State at
this point had no role to play in the secondary education of either girls
or boys. The purpose of the girls 'unprecedented opportunities for
intellectual and physical development . . . and to fit them more
adequately for domestic or professional careers'.[13] Employers could
be confident not only of the educational abilities of those girls
but also of their middle-class origins and respectability. By the
1890s the educational environment was changing. The Technical
Instruction Acts of 1889 and 1891 (using the so-called Whiskey
Money) encouraged local School Boards to develop teaching programmes in commercial subjects. Boys and girls flooded into evening
continuation classes and by 1895 26,222 of them were doing shorthand. Public initiatives supplemented rather than replaced the
technical training in office skills already on offer from a range of
voluntary associations such as the Society of Arts, YMCA, Mechanics
Institutes and local Shorthand Writers Societies. After the 1902
Education Act, State Secondary education was provided for girls and
this went some way to make good the shortage of secondary schools
especially for those girls from less secure middle-class backgrounds
who were eager for secondary education but had previously been
restricted by the School Boards' activities. Building on this base, the
Edwardian years witnessed a substantial increase in the number of
suitably qualified young women who could become clerks.[14] Despite
these advances the progress in girls' secondary and commercial
education had still not gone as far in Britain as in the United States
before the First World War. The American high school system was
more closely geared to the equal schooling of both boys and girls
and this was a key factor in breaking the male monopoly of office work.
The fact that equality of schooling had gone further in the United
States was an important reason why women increased their share of
the American clerical labour force more quickly than they did in
Britain.[15] In 1910, women were already 37·6 per cent of all clerks in

the United States compared with 21·4 per cent of all those in Britain in 1911.

That large numbers of young women educated beyond the elementary level were prepared to forego leisure and invest in evening continuation classes in typewriting and shorthand suggests that wages and other aspects of office work were superior to those in other female occupations. According to data collected by the Cannan Committee of 1909–10 and other sources, female clerks earned on average £1 a week in commerce and rather more in insurance.[16] This compares with an average for all women's wages of between 12 and 14 shillings per week. In manufacturing even the best paid female workers, cotton operatives, earned less than clerks at 18–19 shillings per week. In domestic service, the largest female occupation in this period, cooks employed in the best London households at the turn of the century might earn £25 a year, but the average for London servants was around £18 although most 'lived-in'. Clerical work compared favourably with the narrow range of alternative female white-collar occupations. Hospital nurses, who like clerks were educated beyond the elementary level, earned between £24 and £40 in 1914. Only in school-teaching did women earn substantially higher wages than female clerks. At the top end of the labour market, a very small percentage of female clerks earned higher wages than almost all women and most men. In 1909 six per cent of female commercial clerks earned between £80 and £140 a year, while a very few might earn £3–£4 a week as private secretaries in the top London offices. Only headmistresses in the new state secondary schools earned more than the elite of private secretaries in the top London legal and commercial offices.[17]

Office work also fitted in well with women's expectations of work and of their participation in the labour force. In Victorian Britain, while working-class women often had little choice but to engage in paid work outside the house, this was frowned upon as socially unacceptable for middle-class women. Gentility for such women became linked with dependence. Even before the end of the century, this notion of separate spheres for men and women, although it was still dominant, was coming under pressure. Early feminists publicised the advantage of careers for women, while increasing numbers of women educated beyond the elementary level represented a shift in the potential supply of labour which could hardly be ignored. The characterisation of office work fitted in well with the pursuit of genteel employment. Factory work and domestic service were excluded because they involved manual labour and, apart from being low-paid, were stigmatised by being monopolised by girls from the lower social groups. Apart from the lower professions of nursing and teaching, office work and possibly the higher reaches of shop work were the only occupations widely available which enabled women to be 'ladylike' both in and outside work. The typical Edwardian career girl wanted nothing more than 'a frock-coated something in the city, to live in a suburban semidetached villa and carry a gilt-clasped prayer book to church on Sunday'.[18]

There were more compelling reasons which directed educated young women into office work. Female clerks were young and single before the First World War. In 1911 out of 117,057 female commercial clerks, 114,429 were single and 95 per cent were under the age of thirty-five. Most of these girls probably anticipated working only until marriage. There was a widespread view that the female clerk 'looks on her business life as a few years to be got through as easily and as comfortably to herself as may be until marriage'.[19]

Such attitudes perpetuated the myths of the 'pin money' clerk or of the girls who sought out office work on the chance of marrying the boss. What is certain is that when they did marry, office clerks, like many other working women at this time, other than widows and those with unemployed husbands, left the labour market. The cultural pressures on married women, especially middle-class ones, remaining at home were overwhelming and ensured that careers and marriage did not mix. Of course, many women did not marry at all. There was a large surplus of women in late-Victorian Britain, many of whom were of marriageable age. Among them were educated middle-class girls who were perhaps unlucky and outclassed in the competition for husbands. The emigration of these 'gentlewomen' represented one solution to their predicament, while another was to continue living with and to some extent 'off' their parents, a situation which hinged on the health and earning power of the father. The death of a father forced many educated young women into the labour market. The fictional heroine Juliet Appleton learned typewriting in an East London settlement in the 1890s following her father's death.[20] For these young single women, office work provided the opportunity to follow independent, private and moderately comfortable lives.

The process of feminisation

By 1914 the basis was laid for an expansion in the number of female clerks. This would have occurred even in normal conditions, but two world wars accelerated the process. In 1911 women made up about 21 per cent of Britain's total number of clerks, but in the 1920s and 1930s they had stabilised around 45 per cent and by 1951 they were in a clear majority. The gains in clerical work assume an added significance when set within the wider context of female job opportunities. The overall labour force participation rate of women actually declined slightly between 1911 and 1951; in manufacturing the inter-war years saw the decline of traditional 'women's' industries like textiles.[21] The huge gains made by women in the First World War in munitions and engineering were quickly lost with the return to peace as the industries contracted, as well as in the face of hostility from powerful male trade unions. Office work represented one of the few lasting gains.

Table 1.1 *Clerks and typists in Britain, 1931 and 1951*

| | England and Wales | | Scotland | |
	Male	Female	Male	Female
1931	795,486	579,945	69,272	77,451
1951	861,676	1,270,456	70,485	138,699

Source: Census Returns.

As office workers, women proved more flexible than men in the changing economic conditions of the inter-war years. Their numbers could be increased or decreased with equal ease. In particular, they came to monopolise the routine jobs which formed a virtual secondary labour market in clerical work, often replacing men and boy clerks in the worst years of the slump. Cohn, in his case studies of the Great Western Railway and the Post Office, concluded that among the reasons for the large-scale recruitment of women was the slowdown in the organisational growth of these large institutions in the 1920s, with reduced opportunities for junior male clerks anticipating long careers. The turnover of permanent male staff was low and openings for juniors were drying up. The traditional apprenticeship system for boy clerks could not be sustained and, in any case, many able boys now saw higher education as a superior alternative to clerical work, so that the quality of male applicants was deteriorating. There was a pressing need to fill the low-level, high turnover and temporary jobs such as typists, file clerks and office machine operators and managers, uncertain of the quality or quantity of male applicants and unable to offer long-term careers, turned to women as an ideal alternative.[22] These findings confirm some important contemporary investigations. Klingender believed that female clerks survived the Depression rather better than men and concluded that only 'blind alley' office jobs were available to young men, while Caradog-Jones in his *Social Survey of Merseyside* thought that women were replacing male clerks in Liverpool in the depths of the slump.[23] Female clerks appear to have suffered less from the Depression than men. White-collar workers were generally badly affected, and clerical work became effectively split between permanent and temporary employment. Many mature male clerks, some of whom fell outside the net of state insurance, suffered long-term unemployment and struggled to re-enter the labour market at anything like their previous salary levels because of their age and over-specialisation. In contrast, the demand for typing skills was generally buoyant and women were unlikely to remain unemployed for long. With their more generalised skills they were better able to engage in successful job-searching and in any event were probably more prepared to accept short-term employment.[24]

This flexibility could work in the opposite direction. Women were more easily dispensable than permanent male clerks. Many were recruited as temporary clerks in the First World War and with the return of peace they had to make way for returning men.[25] In addition, they also suffered as employers searched for economies in the face of rising labour costs. The Liverpool-based Union Marine Insurance Company, which as we have already seen was recruiting female clerks before 1914, accelerated this process during the war. By 1921 the company was faced with a rising wage bill caused by the payment of contingent grants to 'top up' the salaries of its male permanent staff to cover the post-war cost-of-living increases. Women were deliberately excluded from these payments. The company achieved its savings partly by pensioning off a few male staff but mainly by dispensing with some thirty-seven female clerks who had been recruited on a temporary basis during the war.[26] Meta Zimmeck shows in this volume how, by the end of the First World War, women were employed in all grades of the Civil Service, but in a reconstruction programme aimed at the needs of returning ex-servicemen and preserving the 'social tone' of the Civil Service for the male mandarins who ran it, they lost heavily both in the number and type of posts available to them.

Table 1.2 *Union Marine Insurance Company staffing levels and salary bills, 1913 and 1921*

Year	Male	Female	Total	Total remuneration (£)
1913	115	11	126	21,582
1921	117	59	176	58,988

Source: Union Marine Insurance Records.

In other ways too the advance of women into clerical work, despite the significant gains, was hampered between the wars. Ever since the first influx of female clerks, employers had practised discriminatory policies against them once they married. This ensured that few women could seriously entertain the notion of careers, marriage and children even if they wished and few probably did so before the First World War. In the 1920s and 1930s, these policies were, if anything, more deeply entrenched. Employers, male-dominated trade unions and even unmarried female clerks colluded to keep married women out of employment. In the private sector, this exclusionary policy tended to be informal but nonetheless universal, while in the public sector it was enforced legally. Trade unions were also stronger in the public sector and even if they admitted women to the membership they were run in the men's interests.[27] In 1931, for example, NALGO agitated successfully for the marriage bar to be maintained in local government. Single women in NALGO were opposed to married women working because their 'pin money' would depress women's pay levels.[28]

Two distinct stocks of qualified female office workers were built up between the wars. There were those who were single and in work, and those who had worked but were now married. During the Second World War, the mobilisation of female labour was even more intensive than in the First, and the pool of office-trained women who had worked before the Second World War were given priority both in the new jobs being created and in reinstatement to jobs which they had previously held. The main gains were in national and local government with women rising to nearly half the workforce, and this employment did not contract as sharply as it had after the First World War. Many women in wartime agencies were transferred to the growing government departments associated with the labour government's post-war welfare programme.[29]

The gains made by married women in office employment in the Second World War formed the basis for their rising share of employment in the post-war service sector. In the years immediately following the war, working women who married continued to be caught in the trap about expectations of their roles as workers and wives. Once they had children they were expected to quit work. However, the situation was changing gradually in their favour. Marriage bars, which had been reinforced in the 1930s Depression, were eroded by the powerful role of married women in the war economy. Formal restrictions were gradually broken down, going in the Civil Service in 1946 but proving more tenacious in the Post Office where they lasted until 1963.[30] More fundamentally, the service revolution continued apace in British society generating a demand for routine office jobs which could no longer be supplied by the pool of spinster clerks and young girls who had dominated the labour market between 1890 and 1950. Finally, office work once again proved its flexibility with the growth of part-time employment which fitted in well with women's other roles as wives and mothers. Interestingly, these changes occurred on both sides of the Atlantic at about the same time. Margaret Hedstrom argues in this volume that prejudices against older married women in the USA after the Second World War were tempered by doubts about the adequacy of both the supply and the quality of younger recruits. Pressures upon employers to utilise the pool of married women eventually overcame their exaggerated fears that they would need regular salary increases, pensions and promotion.[31] Since the Second World War, older married women have to a large extent come to replace older married men in clerical work.

This has been one important effect of a wider process of structural and sectoral changes in the British economy which has strongly favoured the growth of women's employment. Two major economic developments have occurred in post-war Britain, accelerating in the last couple of decades. Firstly there has been a marked loss of employment and security for industrial or manufacturing workers in a range of industries from older staples such as coal and railways to newer ones like motor cars. This process is central to what some observers describe as the de-industrialisation of Britain. Over the same period but building on much older foundations, there has been a major movement of jobs into the white-collar and service sectors. While men have been the major losers from de-industrialisation, women have been the major beneficiaries from the growth of the service sector. Since the war there has been an overall rise in the rate at which women have participated in the labour force with a marked growth in the openings for married and part-time workers. Many of the new service jobs have been dominated by women and office work has been in the vanguard of this process. Whereas before the 1950s, women's gains in clerical work were partly offset by the decline of domestic service and the loss of women's industrial jobs, since then solid gains have been made. As Rosemary Crompton shows in this volume, women have come to dominate office work and it now easily forms the largest single category of female employment. The decline of manufacturing industry has thrown the 'social revolution' associated with female service and white-collar employment into even sharper relief. Indeed, it has had an important impact upon the gender composition of clerical work itself. While those sectors, like transport, coal and manufacturing, where men previously formed a majority of the clerical labour force have declined as employers, the advancing areas of public administration, finance, banking and insurance have been rapidly feminised.[32]

The experience of work

While the aggregate gains made by women in office work are undeniable and impressive, much more controversy centres upon their work experiences inside the office. Some observers have drawn attention to the persistence of gender inequality in the office with regard to pay and promotion. They point to a vertical segmentation of office labour in which men have careers and women are left with the low-paid or low-status jobs. According to this view, these inequalities are not based solely or even mainly upon objective differences between men and women such as level of education, qualifications or proven ability but are part of a patriarchal system in which most jobs are gendered. Jobs associated with responsibilities and opportunities require 'masculine' characteristics such as assertiveness and ambition, while women are expected to fill those which are essentially supportive. Inside the office, while salesmen, office managers and accountants are located on one side of the gender divide, typists, file-clerks and more recently VDU operators monopolise the other.

Historically, there is little doubt that the separation and sub-ordination of women in domestic life was carried over into their working lives. In clerical work the first generation of women workers were widely regarded as little more than 'office wives' or even servants. This servility could be formally structured. The Mersey Dock and Harbour Board, a major employer of white-collar labour in Liverpool, classified only its male white-collar personnel as company 'officers' while the rest, unskilled working-class males and female office workers, were categorised as 'servants'.[33] The first female clerks entered a world not very different from a boys' school or a gentleman's club. As female newcomers they were regarded as something of an oddity and felt themselves to be out of place.

'The middle-class girl, equipped with her skills and typewriting', observed one Edwardian correspondent, 'was often ill-equipped to deal with the male office society. We were educated at home by governesses and had no commercial training, so when circumstances obliged us to turn to and earn a living we felt like fish out of water. It was not until I had been in the office several months till I settled down. I discovered gradually that any newcomer took on average a few weeks and precocious office boys a few days to feel perfectly at home. Why did I feel out of place? This is where a High School training is doubtless of great value to girls in commercial life. The general feeling of esprit de corps which is only acquired in school or perhaps a very large family is precisely similar to the feeling regarding office life. At school, boys and girls constantly grumble at work and teachers but will never allow an outsider to speak scathingly of their school. This is the case in the office.[34]

The difficulties which the correspondent experienced in adjusting to office life may have had more to do with her gender than her education. While women were in a minority in office work they were treated with suspicion and even hostility by many male clerks. They were ridiculed as 'pin money' types and 'husband hunters' and as women who had 'desexed' themselves by entering a male preserve. Psychologically some male clerks may have been on the defensive because the influx of women confirmed doubts about the 'masculinity' of office work. 'Born a man died a clerk' was a long-held view of clerking strongly suggestive that it was not fit work for a man to do at all.[35] And there was a history of ambitious, upwardly-mobile men getting out of clerical work into more rewarding and important careers.

Women provided a convenient scapegoat for more fundamental developments which combined to undermine the position of many clerks at the beginning of the twentieth century. The sheer expansion of numbers associated with the growth of the service sector was a development over which the individualistic and largely ununionised clerks had no control. The skills associated with the Victorian office lost their scarcity value in the face of educational changes and the creation of a more elastic, better-educated labour force. At the same time clerks, socially on the margin, were threatened by a more independent working-class political and trade union movement from one direction and from the decline of their self-made, small-scale paternalistic employers from another. Changes in business organisation, the threat of foreign competition and, between the wars, the reality of depression, cut off clerks' traditional chances of movement into the employer class. Fears of overstocking and undercutting to some extent pre-dated the large scale influx of women in the labour market. In the 1880s they had focused on the invasion of foreign, and especially German clerks, who would accept a nominal wage in order to perfect their English and learn about local business practices. Women were a more enduring scapegoat for labour market changes and loss of status of which they are probably best seen as a symptom rather than a cause.[36]

Whether women were anything more than a scapegoat actually competing with and replacing men is more questionable. Some replacement in certain jobs and at certain times did, of course, occur. The correspondence clerks of Victorian commerce, whose skills of penmanship and letter-writing had placed them in a strategic position in the old counting-house, lost their monopoly in the face of women equipped with technical skills like typewriting. Initially men did train as typists (they had always counted shorthand among their skills) but when it became clear that typists were not likely to be promoted they lost interest and the job was quickly feminised. While women dominated typing from the beginning, their movement into other office jobs has been more gradual. It has taken two forms. Firstly, high-status male jobs such as book-keeping were deskilled and taken over by women. Secondly, men transferred out of low-level office jobs which were filled by women while new routine jobs were created for women from the beginning. In the Victorian office, the book-keeper's job was to record all the transactions but this became more difficult as organisational requirements grew more complex. Over time, the book-keepers' managerial functions were taken over by accountants with responsibilities for financial planning and administration. Beneath the accountants, large numbers of routine 'book-keeping' jobs proliferated which were increasingly mechanised by the introduction of calculating and adding machines and filled by women. In both Britain and the

USA, the feminisation of book-keeping developed between the wars with calculating and book-keeping machines taking their place alongside the typewriter.[37] Women not only filled specific, standardised jobs as machine operators, book-keepers and typists but they were also employed as 'Jills-of-all-trades', routinely handling, processing, recording and filing the huge volume of paper being generated, doing the kind of jobs which office boys and juniors had done in the past. However, the influx of women did not lead to large-scale jobs losses among men. Unemployment caused by direct substitution has occurred only in exceptional conditions. In the 1930s, in both Britain and the USA, male clerks were replaced by women in the depths of the slump while unemployed, but previously well-placed, mature men were forced to compete with women for the most routine jobs rather than endure the stigma of unemployment.[38]

In general, men who have been replaced by women have been redeployed within the office hierarchy. In fact, the feminisation of office work has coincided with, and contributed to, the continuous and major reclassification of office jobs in ways which have led to the large-scale vertical segregation of men and women. Since the nineteenth century, employers have experimented with the classification of their clerks in ways which could accommodate the impact of women, mechanisation, provision of careers for men, increases in scale and the application of methods of 'scientific management'. The main effect of this process has been that (most) men have moved into superior career-based grades, while women have been allocated low-level jobs with few opportunities for promotion. Sylvia Walby has recently argued that vertical segregation was part of a deliberate strategy in the first phase of feminisation, with employers placating male fears over displacement by segregating women into jobs which did not compete with them.[39] By the inter-war years, the internal division of labour in the office was organised along these lines. A few examples will suffice. In Liverpool's Mersey, Dock and Harbour Board the reclassification of clerks in the 1920s (one of many), placed women in a separate and inferior category to men. While men had progressive careers stretching from junior, through second and up to first grade clerks, women were in a single category. Only two women were in the ungraded office category, which would have made them eligible for higher salaries on account of special duties.[40] In 1936, the Association of Female Clerks and Secretaries discovered that some firms employed only women as shorthand typists and machine operators, while others employed only men on accounts, costing and statistical work.[41] Segmentation occurred even within the same occupation. Both men and women worked as book-keepers, but it was the women who performed the manual and mechanical tasks while men conceptualised and supervised these tasks. Since the Second World War the process of segmentation has been largely maintained. Women have continued their monopoly of typing and form a majority among the other office machine operators, including the large number of VDU operators. While mechanisation has reinforced and highlighted gender segmentation, the process has been occurring among other office jobs. Since the 1950s, as Rosemary Crompton shows in this volume, women have come to form a majority of clerks other than typists and are employed on a wide range of less-specialised duties which often vary considerably between firms. Even those described as typists or machine operators have always been expected to turn their hands to other tasks. These routine jobs were once filled by men and indeed, the process of feminisation has been slower here as men held on to these jobs temporarily while on the way up the career hierarchy. Finally, rigid segmentation has been closely linked to bureaucratisation and has been a characteristic of large rather than small organisations. In the past, it was commonplace in local and central government when 'women only' grades were created, partly in the face of hostility from male-dominated trade unions. In response, female clerks formed their own separate trade unions.[42]

Despite women's difficulties in developing successful careers in the office, various forms of mobility have actually occurred. From the beginning, women have exploited the clerical labour market to their own advantage. Information about variations in pay and conditions have always circulated widely among women through their trade unions, employment agencies, social clubs or simply by 'word of mouth'. If movement within firms was difficult, movement between them was easier. The existence of a large temporary sector in women's office work has also increased mobility. Women have shown much less reluctance than men to accept temporary office work and, equipped with their generalised skills of typing, shorthand and, more recently, word processing, they have been strategically placed to do so. Between the wars while unemployed, over-specialised male clerks struggled to find jobs at all, the demand for female typists was high, even if many jobs were temporary. Women readily took these jobs in order to requalify for benefits. More recently, some young women have been seeking temporary jobs as a preferred alternative to permanent ones, maximising their incomes in tight labour markets. In the London of the 1980s, these freelance 'super temps' have been described as 'office adventurers ... the secretarial equivalent of the highflyers in the City of London'.[43]

When upward mobility within offices has occurred, it has generally meant the supervision of women rather than men. The physical separation and segregation of women from men in some of the early offices created the need for supervisors who, on moral and practical grounds (they cost less), had to be women. The reorganisation and rationalisation of office labour, notably the creation of 'pools' of female clerks and typists, has had a similar effect. In the larger offices after the First World War, girls went out to the departmental managers to take dictation before returning to the pool to do their transcription, under the watchful eye of a lady superintendent who it was said 'studies practical psychology and knows how to manage the girls'.[44] Since the Second World War this supervisory group, broadly defined, has expanded as a proportion of the female clerical workforce, although the movement of men into senior positions has been far more impressive and complete. Feminists have strongly criticised the female supervisors as occupying a kind of 'no-man's land' in the office, both isolated from the clerical ranks and cut off from the higher grades which are normally reserved for men.[45] While this group should not be regarded as part of the male executive stratum, they do represent the first level of management and the gains though modest are increasing and should not be underestimated.[46]

Jobs as high-flying personal assistants or private secretaries represent another form of career mobility. Private secretaries have always been paid higher wages than their rank-and-file sisters and were better educated, probably knew foreign languages and entered the superior business house where they worked shorter hours and rarely did overtime. Between the wars, these women found new employment in discount houses and the local offices of foreign banks but male correspondence clerks were still preferred in shipping offices because they were suitable for clerkships abroad.[47] It is among such women that the image of the glamorous career girl has grown, often successfully cultivated by male executives intent on personalising their staff.[48] Bosses do delegate increasingly to their private secretaries who may also have access to confidential information, both of which are sources of organisational power. However, the private secretary's status and pay depends on the success of her boss, rising and falling in line with his. The introduction of 'typing pools' was one way in which companies replaced private secretaries and extended their control over their executives.[49] In any event, even high-flying secretaries know that there is little scope for entering management and some see a move sideways into high-paying temporary jobs as a substitute for upward mobility.[50]

Figure 1.1 *Male (M) and Female (F) clerical employment: senior and junior grades, Great Britain, 1951–1981*

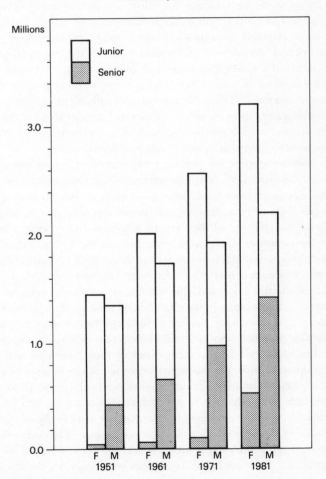

Despite limited promotion prospects, office work has remained an attractive employment for women. The physical conditions of work have improved dramatically over the last half century. In the past, many offices were ill-ventilated places without separate sanitary accommodation, forcing female employees to rely 'on the ABC shops and railway stations'.[51] The presence of women probably forced employers in the interests of propriety to improve office accommodation, thus benefiting men as well as women. Even before the First World War, new purpose-built offices included separate facilities. Clerks' trade unions fought hard for the improvement of work conditions and the inclusion of offices in factory and workshop legislation, but many female clerks preferred to trust to their employers and were opposed to legislation which might exclude them from shiftwork and 'shut them out from employment in the largest offices'.[52] Occupational illnesses associated with office work are not unknown, ranging from strain arising from typing to more recent worries about transmissions from VDUs.[53] But women are unlikely to sustain serious or disabling injuries in the office, which must be regarded as safer and more pleasant workshops than factories, shops or domestic households where women have traditionally been employed.

In another respect too the work experience of female clerks has probably improved. Working women have always had to contend with sexual advances from men, who have been unable to distinguish between their roles as females and as workers. Many women have accepted the spillover of their female role into the workplace as the price for inclusion in the workforce. Indeed, the first female clerks actively promoted their femininity as an asset which employers should exploit. 'It will be a sorrowful time indeed for this country', wrote a female shorthand writer in 1906, 'when women become men and men women . . . The woman in the office has no need to be anything but a woman . . . Women have purified the office morally and otherwise.'[54] The visible presence of women in the office created the opportunity for sexual exploitation and was made easier by their largely subordinate role in the workforce. Parents were warned to inquire into the business lives of their daughters because the 'downward course is so easy particularly in an office where the clerk's duties bring her into a closer relationship with her employer than that of her sister in the workroom permits'.[55] Often it was a case of 'submit or get out'. The vulnerability of women to sexual harassment within the closed world of the paternalistic counting-house corresponded closely to the dangers facing female servants in domestic households. One effect of the gradual shift in the last fifty years from the small counting-house to the larger, bureaucratised office has been the creation of a more regulated and safer environment for women. This has also been matched in recent years by a greater preparedness to deal with sexual harassment by individual women, their trade unions and employers.[56]

Despite continued discrimination in pay and promotion, office work remains among the most attractive of all jobs available to women. Job satisfaction among female clerks is considerably higher than among female manual workers and the social rewards of office work are considerable, especially the creation of friendships among colleagues in a congenial environment. However, if career success appears as less central in women's than in men's lives, this may be because women have had to scale down their ambitions to match the realities of the workplace.[57] In employment terms, female office workers have proved to be more resistant to business fluctuations than their manual counterparts. They have been relatively untouched by periods of high unemployment as in the 1930s and 1980s, and if they did lose their jobs they were able to re-enter the labour market faster than other workers. Finally, although technological change and office reorganisation have been essential components of the process of feminisation, fears have been voiced recently about technological unemployment arising out of the shift towards the so-called paperless office. As the most dramatic technological changes in the history of office work are happening now, the long-term effects on women's employment remain uncertain, but the introduction of micro-computers has not so far led to any overall reduction in job opportunities or to loss of earnings.[58]

Notes

1 Data from A. H. Halsey, *Tends in British Society since 1900*, London, 1972, p. 114 and E. J. Rotella, 'The transformation of the American office: changes in employment and technology', *Journal of Economic History*, Vol. XLI, No. 1, 1981, p. 52.

2 For a fuller description of Munby's contacts with female clerks in mid-Victorian London, see Chapter 3.

3 For accounts of the old counting-house world, see G. Anderson, *Victorian Clerks*, Manchester University Press, 1976, and D. Lockwood, *The Blackcoated Worker*, London, 1958.

4 Figures used throughout are from the census which were gathered together by Robert Ward, Research Officer in the Department of Economics, University of Salford. I would like to take this opportunity of thanking Mr Ward for his help in the collection and collation of the occupational data.

5 Union Marine Insurance Records, Secretary's Report on the Staff 1904, Merseyside County Archives.

6 *The Shorthand Writer,* November 1986.

7 B. L. Hutchins, 'An enquiry into the salaries and hours of typists and shorthand writers', *The Economic Journal,* Vol. XVI, 1906.

8 D. C. Jones *et al.* (eds.), *The Social Survey of Merseyside,* Liverpool, 1934, Vol. II, p. 326.

9 See E. J. Rotella, 'Women's Labour Force Participation and the Growth of Clerical Employment in the USA', PhD, Department of Economics, University of Pennsylvania, p. 209.

10 On the provision of instruction by the early typewriter companies, see Margaret Mulvihill, 'The White-Bloused Revolution', unpublished MA Research dissertation, University of London, 1981.

11 Olive P. Rayner, *The Typewriter Girl,* London, 1891, p. 27.

12 *Handbook of Employment in Liverpool,* Liverpool Education Committee, 1916, p. 173.

13 K. E. McCrane, 'Play up! Play up and play the game, sports at the late Victorian girls' public school', *Journal of British Studies,* Vol. XXIII, No. 2, 1984.

14 On the changing background of public and private provision of commercial education, see Gladys Carnaffan's essay in this volume which focuses on the role of Skerry's colleges. See also Anderson, *Victorian Clerks,* Chapter 6.

15 See C. Goldin, 'The historical evolution of female earnings, functions and occupations', *Explorations in Economic History,* Vol. 21, 1984, pp. 1–27.

16 The Cannan Committee collected data on male and female clerks by industry. Quoted in F. E. Klingender, *The Condition of Clerical Labour in England,* London, 1935, p. 20.

17 Wages for other female workers are derived from a variety of sources, but see especially L. Holcombe, *Victorian Ladies at Work, Middle-Class Working Women in England and Wales 1850–1914,* Newton Abbot, 1973.

18 *The Woman Worker,* 24 March 1909.

19 *The Business Girl,* February 1912.

20 Rayner, *Typewriter Girl,* p. 17.

21 See J. E. Cronin, *Labour and Society in Britain 1918–1979,* Batsford Academic, London, 1984, pp. 54–5, and E. Roberts, *Women's Work 1840–1940,* Studies in Economic and Social History, London, 1988.

22 S. Cohn, *The Process of Occupational Sex-Typing, The Feminization of Clerical Labor in Great Britain,* Temple University Press, Philadelphia, 1985.

23 See Klingender, *Condition,* pp. 95–6, and D. C. Jones, *Social Survey,* Vol. II, p. 326.

24 See G. Anderson, 'A private welfare agency for white-collar workers between the wars, a study of the Liverpool Clerks' Association 1918–1939', *International Review of Social History,* Vol. XXXI, 1986, part 1, pp. 34–5.

25 On the impact of the two world wars on female clerical employment, see G. Braybon and P. Summerfield, *Out of the Cage, Women's Experiences in two World Wars,* Pandora Press, London, 1987. On the losses in the civil service following the First World War, see M. Zimmeck, 'Strategies and strategems for the employment of women in the British civil service, 1919–1939,' *The Historical Journal,* Vol. 27, No. 4, 1984, pp. 901–24. See also S. Walby, *Patriarchy at Work,* Polity Press, Oxford, 1986, pp. 164–6, 198.

26 Union Marine Insurance Record, Staff Head Office and Branches, Merseyside County Archives.

27 On the persistence and effectiveness of marriage bars see Cohn, *Process of Occupational Sex-Typing*.

28 For NALGO's activities, see S. Boston, *Women Workers and Trade Unions*, London, 1980, p. 164.

29 See Boston, *Women Workers*, p. 203, and P. Summerfield, *Women Workers in the Second World War*, London, 1984.

30 See Walby, *Patriarchy*, p. 198.

31 See Chapter 7 and the recent excellent surveys of female office workers in the USA in H. I. Hartmann *et al.*, *Computer Chips and Paper Clips*, National Academy Press, Washington, 1986, and H. I. Hartmann (ed.), *Technology and Women's Employment*, National Academy Press, Washington, 1987.

32 On the extension of women into office jobs other than typing since the Second World War, see Chapter 6. J. Cronin, *Labour and Society*, has interesting thoughts on the juxtaposition of de-industrialisation and the service revolution.

33 Mersey Docks and Harbour Board, Lists of Officers, Merseyside County Archives.

34 *The Woman Worker*, 23 October 1908.

35 See M. Zimmeck, 'Jobs for the girls: the expansion of clerical work 1850–1914', in A. V. John (ed.), *Unequal Opportunities, Woman's Employment in England 1800–1918*, Oxford, 1986.

36 On the insensitivity among male clerks before the First World War, see G. Anderson, *Victorian Clerks*, pp. 60–5.

37 On the feminisation of book-keeping see S. H. Strom, ' "Machines instead of clerks", technology and the feminisation of book-keeping, 1910–1950', in H. I. Hartmann (ed.), *Technology and Women's Employment*.

38 For the impact of the inter-war slump on clerical labour in Britain, see G. Anderson, 'A private welfare agency', and for the USA see S. H. Strom, "Machines instead of clerks".

39 See S. Walby, *Patriarchy at Work*, pp. 152–5.

40 Mersey, Docks and Harbour Board, Minutes of Finance Committee, 3 July 1920, Merseyside County Archives.

41 Association of Women Clerks and Secretaries, Annual Report, 31 December 1936.

42 In the civil service women broke away from male trade unions which failed to support their demands and set up their own Federation of Women Clerks and Secretaries. See S. Walby, *Patriarchy*, p. 187. In the private sector the Association of Women Clerks and Secretaries was a breakaway from the National Union of Clerks.

43 On the mobility of women between firms before 1914, see M. Zimmeck, 'Jobs for the girls', pp. 166–8. The large temporary sector of men and women between the wars is covered in G. Anderson, 'A private welfare agency', pp. 33–4, and for the lifestyle of the mobile 'super-temp' in contemporary London, see 'Girls in the big city' in the *Sunday Telegraph*, 12 April 1987.

44 'Are girl clerks efficient?' *Liverpool Daily Post*, 22 February 1921.

45 For a critical view of the role of female office supervisors, see E. N. Glenn and R. L. Feldberg, 'Degraded and deskilled, the proletariatisation of clerical work', in R. Kahn-Hut *et al.*, *Women and Work: Problems and Perspectives*, Oxford University Press, 1982, p. 212.

46 I am grateful to Robert Ward for the processing of data on junior/senior ratios. The definitions are as far as possible in terms of the 1951 Census, when local authority officials, Civil Service Executive Officers and Higher Clerical personnel were included in Administration. By 1981 the administration category, apart from senior staff in local government and the Civil Service, include a more detailed breakdown of private sector managers and supervisors of clerks, many of whom are female.

47 D. W. Hughes, *Careers for Daughters*, London, 1936, p. 84.

48 See D. Reisman, *The Lonely Crowd*, Yale University Press, 1961, pp. 264–6.

49 See E. N. Glenn and R. L. Feldburg, 'Degraded and deskilled', pp 204, 212.

50 See 'Girls in the big city', *Sunday Telegraph*, 22 April 1987.

51 Report of Inquiry into the conditions of the typing profession in *The Women's Industrial News*, June 1898.

52 The Typewriting Industry, *The Englishwoman's Review*, 15 July 1902.

53 Pulmonary tuberculosis was a major killer of male clerks before the First World War and women who worked in small, cramped offices must have been equally vulnerable. See G. Anderson, *Victorian Clerks*, pp. 17–19. More recently the syndrome known as 'building sickness' is receiving great publicity and women are more likely to experience it than men. See *Daily Telegraph*, 20 May 1987.

54 Woman's Role in Shorthand, *The Shorthand Writer*, July 1906.

55 See 'Business girl's temptations' in *Liverpool Evening Express*, 10 March 1911. Juliet Appleton, heroine of the *Typewriter Girl*, left her first job because she sensed her boss was about to make advances. See also M. Meyer *et al.*, *Sexual Harrassment*, Petrocelli Books, 1981, USA.

56 On the greater safety in large offices and organisations see M. Zimmeck, 'Jobs for the girls', p. 166 and J. E. Cronin, *Labour and Society*, p. 156.

57 For a recent survey of job satisfaction among manual and non-manual working women, see R. Martin and J. Wallace, *Working in Recession*, Oxford University Press, 1984. See also V. F. Niera and B. A. Gutek, *Women and Work, A Psychological Perspective*, New York, 1981, pp. 61–8, 109–13, which suggests that women may scale down their ambitions at work.

58 See W. W. Daniel, *Workplace Industrial Relations and Technological Change*, Blackmore Press, Dorset, 1987, Chapter 3.

2 Jane E. Lewis

Women clerical workers in the late nineteenth and early twentieth centuries

Thinking about women's work

It is hard to think of jobs that are not gendered, even though what is classified as a male or female job has changed considerably. As M. Stacey has perceived, there have been two quite unrelated theories about the division of labour: 'one that it all began with Adam Smith and the other that it all began with Adam and Eve. The first has to do with production and the social control of workers and the second with reproduction and the social control of women. The problem is that the two accounts, both men's accounts, have never been reconciled.[1]' The task of explaining sexual divisions has only been taken up recently, with the explanation being welded not altogether successfully onto existing theories.

In recent years, major economic theories of human behaviour have paid attention to the sexual division of labour and have stressed the importance of relating women's market work to their familial roles, emphasising the importance of sex roles within the family as determinants of the division of labour in market work. In so doing, they have tended to privilege paid work. Thus neoclassicists have taken the domestic division of labour for granted and have concentrated on the way in which it explains sexual segregation and low pay in market work, while marxists have got bogged down on the question of whether domestic labour is productive work. Both these major theories have tried to incorporate analysis of sexual divisions into their existing theoretical frameworks, but with varying degrees of success.

The 'new home economics' of neoclassical theory recognised that adult married women in particular allocate their time in more complex ways than men – in unpaid non-market work of caring and household labour, as well as in leisure and waged work. It has been argued that because marriage is voluntary, the theory of preferences may readily be applied: wives will hire husbands as breadwinners, and husbands wives as childbearers, minders and housekeepers. The division of labour in the family is assumed to be a natural corollary of women's reproductive role. Because of their childbearing and child-rearing activities (which again are assumed to be naturally linked), married women are held to be imperfect substitutes for men in market work. Women's expectations of marriage and children are held to make them less willing to invest in education and more prone to labour market behaviour that is unstable from the employers point of view. The sexual division of labour is thus 'naturally' complementary and maximises the gains of both partners.[2]

Marxists have also argued that the sexual division of labour may well maximise family welfare, but while neoclassicists argue that the division of labour is a matter of rational choice, marxists see it as one of the few strategies available to the working class in its struggle with capital. Marxists also emphasise the inherent conflict between married women's two roles at home and in waged work and point to the dramatic recent increase in the divorce rate and in the number of single parent families as evidence of increasing tension between the two roles.[3] In the recent literature which attempts to understand the labour market under late capitalism, radical dual labour market theorists suggest that labour markets are divided into primary and secondary sectors, with restricted mobility between the two, by a process of deskilling. Men are thus the passive beneficiaries of capitalist strategy, dominating the primary job sector where employment is relatively stable, higher paid and tied to career ladders, while women are confined to the secondary sector of temporary and poorly paid work.[4]

Thus both major bodies of theory tend to treat work in the family and work in the labour market dichotomously, despite the recognition of important linkages between them, and more often than not, women's position in the family is invoked to explain their position in the labour market. Thus neoclassicists emphasise the importance of choice and argue essentially that women's position reflects the nature of the choices that women make. Radical dual labour market theorists blame capital, but in the end are, like neoclassicists, forced back on female biology to explain why it is women who find themselves in a subordinate position.

Radical feminists have got over this problem in invoking patriarchy to explain the sexual division of labour, arguing that men as capitalists, as husbands and as trade unionists control women, keeping their wages low and enforcing their responsibilities for domestic work.[5] This tends to characterise women as victims and thus oversimplifies the construction and maintenance of the sexual division of work. Rather, it is necessary to take a step back and reconceptualise women's work (in both private and public spheres) as part of the larger gender order, which dictates that men and women have unequal access to resources of all kinds, and that gendered jobs are part of the construction of masculinity and femininity.

Single and married women in different social classes have combined different mixes of paid and unpaid work at different times. In the mid-nineteenth century, married and single working-class women worked outside the home in occupations segregated from men, albeit that the definition of what was a male and female job changed significantly over time. Married working-class women increasingly withdrew from the labour market in the late nineteenth and early twentieth centuries. They retained primary responsibility for home and family, but also often engaged in casual paid employment, much of which escaped the notice of the census enumerators. Both married and single middle-class women were much more firmly excluded from paid employment; their work in the public sphere being largely confined to unpaid voluntary philanthropic effort. It is of course only since the Second World War that married women's employment has increased dramatically. These experiences must be located within a broader gender order in which the law denied women access to property and political rights, and the marriage contracts often resulted in an unequal division of resources and a particular allocation of roles and responsibilities.

Broadly speaking therefore, there has been a shift over time whereby women have increasingly entered the public sphere of paid work, but have retained primary responsibility for domestic work. There has been relatively little change in the domestic division of labour. Recent research has questioned early linear models of development, from segregated sex roles to the modern 'symmetrical family'[6], and has revealed on the one hand evidence of a deeply based home culture in particular regions by the early twentieth century, with men sharing some domestic tasks and caring, and on the other, evidence of the persistence of profoundly separate and antagonistic male and female worlds.[7] It is generally true that even when domestic work has become more equally shared, it still remains primarily women's responsibility. It is clearly the case that women as well as men have tended to see family responsibilities predominating and paid work as secondary to family responsibilities.

Within the sphere of paid work, women's jobs have been segregated from those of men, with the vast majority of women engaged in some kind of human service work. Just as it is important to understand the ways in which women have combined different mixes of paid and unpaid work at different times, it is also important to recognise the way in which much of the work women do has moved in and out of the private sphere. The preparation of meals for school children, for example, has been at different times predominantly unpaid work or part-time paid work, but always women's work.

It is therefore crucial to see the gendering of work in relation not just to changes in the labour process and the economy, but also to the way in which separate male and female work identities have been constructed. It will be argued below that the latter is a complicated process involving consideration of male behaviour as capitalists, trade unionists and husbands, and of women's behaviour as wives and mothers and paid workers.

In the case of clerical work, the increase in demand for clerks in the late nineteenth century and the possession of equivalent skills of the young men and women emerging from the new state elementary schools, meant that men as employers could contemplate employing women who were of course also a cheaper source of labour. But women were not hired *en masse* to replace male clerks. The process of feminisation was slow. Moreover, women were, from the outset, largely confined to their own grades and departments. Male employers and male trade unionists both wanted to minimise the competition between male and female workers. There is not yet sufficient empirical research to determine exactly how this was accomplished in the wide variety of settings in which clerks of various kinds were employed. After outlining the broad patterns of male and female employment in relation to white-collar work, this chapter will merely suggest two lines of interpretation that may be tested further. First, that men as employers and as trade unionists shared particular ideas as to sexual difference and what might be considered appropriate work for women. In the case of employers, these cultural beliefs as to women's role proved stronger than any rational economic urge to rapidly employ the cheapest labour available.[8] Additionally, the segregation of women into particular grades and jobs also served to mollify male clerks, who feared female competition. At present the evidence is not sufficient to be sure of the patterns of causation. Walby has recently argued that it was primarily a case of employers responding to the pressure of male dominated unions for sexual segregation,[9] but from an in-depth study of the Post Office and the Great Western Railway, Cohn has concluded that trade unions exercised little power and that management decisions were the most important in determining sex-typing.[10] I would suggest that the shared concept – between male employers and employees and women – of the labour market behaviour appropriate to women and to men was also important. Second, it is important to consider the expectations, choices and experiences of the women clerks themselves. It is not sufficient to see women as the victims of a particular set of strategies devised by male employers and trade unionists. The life of early twentieth-century single women clerks, living away from home and subsisting on buns and tea was far from pleasant, yet the work was attractive to them not least because it accorded with their own ideas of what was appropriate work. Furthermore, it is likely that a majority did not question the routine nature of the work expected of them or the lack of opportunities for promotion.

The process of feminisation of clerical work

During the twentieth century the female participation rate and the proportion of workers who were women increased steadily (Table 2.1).

Table 2.1 *Participation rates[1]: Males and females, England and Wales, 1901–81*

Year	Males	Females	Women as % of labour force
1901[2]	837	316	29·1
1911[2]	838	325	29·7
1921[3]	871	323	29·5
1931[4]	905	342	29·7
1951[5]	875	349	30·8
1961	862	377	32·5
1971	814	428	36·5
1981[6]	777	454	38·7

Notes: 1 Number in labour force per 1,000 in each category.
2 Persons aged 10 or over.
3 Persons aged 12 or over.
4 Persons aged 14 or over.
5 Persons aged 15 or over.
6 Persons aged 16 or over.
N.B. There is no Census information for 1941.

Sources: C. Hakim, *Occupational Segregation*, Research Paper No. 9, Table 13 (London, Dept. of Employment, 1979), p. 25; 1981 Population Census Report.

For the most part, the increase reflected the entry of more young, single women into the workforce. Between 1871 and 1881 the participation rates of women between 15 and 24 showed a general absolute increase and after 1881 women aged 20–34 increased their participation relative to men of the same age. While after 1921, married women showed a greater tendency to work up to the birth of their first child, married women's participation rate remained about

10 per cent until after the Second World War. Furthermore in white collar occupations, such as clerical work, women were usually required to resign on marriage until the war.

Throughout the period, women were concentrated in certain 'women's jobs'. Table 2.2 shows that in 1901, 54 per cent of women were working in occupations in which 80 per cent or more of all employees were female. In 1971, 44 per cent of women workers were still in such occupations.

Table 2.2 *Women working in occupations (%) by % of women workers in that occupation, England and Wales, 1901–71*

	Women workers in occupations with		
	100% women	*>80% women*	*>60% women*
1901	11	54	74
1911	3	50	68
1921	0·1	48	61
1931	0·1	52	69
1951	0·3	39	64
1961	0	32	56
1971	0	44	75

Source: C. Hakim, *Occupational Segregation*, Research Paper No. 9, Table 12, p. 24.

Women in the 'professional and technical' category were mostly teachers and nurses, and those in the 'commercial and financial' group were mostly shop assistants. By 1951, a dramatic shift had taken place from the traditional late nineteenth-century areas of women's work, particularly domestic service, the clothing trade and the textile industry, to the clerical and typing sector. The decline in the number of servants was particularly great between 1939 and 1948, reflecting in large part the increased demand for women clerks and typists. The number of women working in local and central government increased almost fourfold during these years.

The shift to 'white-blouse' work was the major feature of the change in the occupational distribution of women workers during the period. Lee Holcombe has shown that while the number of women engaged in such work (mainly teaching, retailing, office work and nursing) increased by 161 per cent between 1881 and 1911, the number working in manufacturing industry and domestic service increased by only 24 per cent.[11] Furthermore, the expansion of the non-manual sector was more than twice as rapid for women as for men. In the case of clerical work, while the number of male clerks continued to increase steadily, the growth in the number of women was dramatic (Table 2.3).

It is not until 1951 that the Census shows women clerks outnumbering men; between 1921 and 1961 the number of women office workers increased threefold from just over half to nearly two million. However the writing was very much on the wall by the First World War, and briefly during the war women predominated. For example, in the civil service women numbered 66,000 or 23 per cent in 1914

Table 2.3 *Number of clerks employed, male and female, England and Wales, 1861–1981*

Year	Males	Females	Women as % of clerks employed
1861	91,733	279	0·3
1871	129,271	1,446	1·1
1881	229,705	6,420	2·7
1891	351,486	18,947	5·1
1901	461,164	57,736	11·1
1911	561,155	124,843	18·1
1921	687,121	591,741	46·1
1931	696,662	569,850	45·0
1951	861,679	1,270,456	59·6
1961	994,810	1,780,190	64·2
1971	822,160	2,119,490	72·1
1981	672,250	2,342,570	77·7

Note: The detailed census classification of occupations differs for each census, and clerical occupations seem to have posed particular difficulties for census officials. As a consequence the figures presented for each of the above censuses have had to be developed independently, and while they accurately reflect the trends in clerical employment exact inter-censal comparison is uncorrected.

Sources: Lee Holcombe, *Victorian Ladies at Work* (Hamden Conn, Archon Books, 1973), p. 210, Table 4a; Population Census Reports, England and Wales, 1921–81.

and 225,000 or 55 per cent in 1918, working primarily in clerical grades, but also in most men's classes in most departments.[12] The number of women employed as clerks was dramatically reduced immediately after the War, reflecting, as Table 2.1 shows, the overall pattern in women's employment. The trend towards the employment of women office workers was not reversed for long, but the experience of widespread female employment during the war helps to explain the determination on the part of employers and clerical unions after it was over to secure devices, such as an intensification of the marriage bar, that would protect male employees from female competition and secure male career paths.

Recent analysis has shown how women's work has and continues to be, segregated from that of men. Table 2.2 shows how the vast majority of women were confined to a very few occupational sectors – what Catherine Hakim has termed horizontal segregation.[13] The entry of women into clerical work threatened substantially to shift the boundary between what was considered male and female jobs. Not surprisingly, male clerks at the end of the nineteenth and beginning of the twentieth century protested. One wrote to the *Liverpool Echo* in 1911 to suggest that:

These intrepid 'typewriter pounders' instead of being allowed to gloat over love novels or do fancy crocheting during the time they are not 'pounding' should fill in their spare time washing out the offices and dusting same, which you will no doubt agree is more suited to their sex and maybe would give them a little practice and insight into the work they will be called upon to do should they so far demean themselves as to marry one of the poor male clerks whose living they are doing their utmost to take out of his hands at the present time.[14]

The broad trend in the figures on the relative positions of male and female clerical workers would suggest that the men were correct in their fears. To all intents and purposes, clerical work became increasingly feminised and deskilled during the twentieth century. Furthermore, as this happened the wages of male clerks suffered considerable decline, while those of female clerks, whose wages were less than half those of men before the First World War showed a marginal increase.[15]

However, the picture is considerably more complicated than this general pattern suggests. In the first place, clerical work is not a homogenous category. Prior to the First World War, over 90 per cent of female clerks employed in the private sector were to be found in commercial and business premises, the inferior end of the office work hierarchy. There were very few in banks, insurance or the railways. In the civil service in 1911, women were concentrated in the Post Office, where they worked as telegraphists and telephone operators and clerks. A 1910 official inquiry found three classes of women clerk: at the top the better educated shorthand typist with perhaps a foreign language would earn £2–£4 a week. In better class business houses, a woman might earn 20–30 shillings, but the vast majority went to work straight out of elementary school at the age of 14 and did no better than a domestic servant or a woman in a low paid manufacturing occupation, such as clothing or the metal trades, earning 10–15 shillings a week.[16]

From the beginning, therefore, women were for the most part confined to the lowest status jobs and within any particular organisation they were segregated in terms of job classification and usually physically separated from male workers. The civil service example is the best documented. In 1881 a grade of women clerks was opened in the Post Office and in 1883, a grade of women sorters; neither mixed with male workers. Another department reported in 1889 that it had set up:

a separate room and convenience . . . which would leave the ladies completely to themselves and free from any danger of interference. We have got two young women at (I think) 23s. and 21s. a week and they do their work excellently. I think they turn out as much work as four copyists could do . . . The women are excellent and give no trouble.[17]

Women clerks were effectively ghettoised in their own grades and departments. Shorthand clerks or typists had no means of promotion. Even as physical segregation broke down and women and men worked alongside each other, the different classifications persisted and survived the rationalisation and fragmentation of clerical work and the creation and destruction of jobs.[18] As Anderson has noted, by 1900 it was clear that women would not threaten the well-placed male career clerk.[19]

During the long process of 'feminisation', first, substantial new white-collar employment opportunities opened up for men, in, for example, accounting, sales and office management, and second, some sort of promotion ladder was made available to the majority of men who continued to enter clerkdom. Rosemary Crompton and Gareth Jones have recently argued that the deskilling of clerical work has been mediated for men by the creation of low paid, low status female internal labour markets; the male career path thus being preserved at the expense of women. Crompton and Jones' analysis is not primarily historical, but it provides the best starting point for any explanation of women's position in clerical work over time.[20] Despite his belief that clerical work was not deskilled before the Second World War, Cohn agrees that employers used strategies relating to the gendering of the workforce that were crucial to maintaining segmented reward systems.[21] The following sections of this chapter are designed to explore how men legitimised such a strategy and the extent to which it proved acceptable to women. This is not a simple tale of male 'conspiracy'. The quotations above also reveal male ideas as to women's proper place and anxiety about the morality of mixing the sexes in the workplace. These reflected the dominant scientific and cultural beliefs of the day and were in large part shared by women themselves.

Men's views of the position of women clerks

When women were first employed within the civil service as tele-graphists, the advantages of employing them were well understood and explicitly stated:

In the first place, they have in an eminent degree the quickness of eye and ear, the delicacy of touch, which are essential qualifications of a good operator.

In the second place, they take more kindly than men or boys do to sedentary employment, and are more patient during long confinement to one place.

In the third place, the wages, which would draw male operators from but an inferior class of the community, will draw female operators from a superior class.[22]

The official added that women were additionally less liable to join trade unions to demand higher wages and, because they would get married, they would not become eligible for the incremental increases in salary expected by established civil servants. In this statement are joined the two staples of employers arguments in favour of the employment of women clerks: first that they were cheap, and second, that they were possessed of secondary sexual characteristics that rendered them particularly suitable for routine work. The latter argument also served to restrict the sort of work considered suitable for women.

Late Victorian social theory drew a firm line between the public and private spheres and enforced the division most firmly in the case of middle-class women. While middle-class men, as Olive Schreiner bitterly observed, had no hesitation in relying on the arduous work of their female domestic servants,[23] they had no intention of permitting either their wives or daughters to engage in paid employment. In the view of Herbert Spencer, the idealised 'angel of the home' represented the perfectly evolved woman.[24] The idea that there was a 'natural' basis for sexual difference, as opposed to patently artificial class differences, was powerful and long-lived. As the prominent physician, Henry Maudsley put it in 1874, 'sex is fundamental, lies deeper than culture, (and) cannot be ignored or defied with impunity'.[25] Arguments regarding biologically based sexual differences applied to all women, but the Victorian scientists who developed them built their theories on the basis of assumptions regarding the behaviour of women of their own class. As Elizabeth Fee has pointed out, there was therefore an essential circularity in their reasoning.[26] They used their own society as the model from which they formulated their ideas, which in turn justified the position of women as they found it. It was not of course the wives and daughters of middle-class men who comprised the majority of women entering clerical work, although as the Post Office official quoted above observed, early applicants tended to be of a higher social class than their male equivalents. For middle-class women without a male protector, clerical work appeared particularly attractive in an extremely limited labour market.

Employers would have agreed that women's place was ideally in the home and that men had both more right and a greater obligation to engage in paid employment, because of their responsibility to keep a family. Thus despite women's cheapness and, by the First World War, their proven capacity, employers in the Civil Service had no hesitation in giving preference to male ex-servicemen, despite the fact that it was estimated that only 20 per cent approached the standard required.[27] Furthermore, these ex-servicemen remained permanently in temporary posts and provided the pool from which the clerical grades of the Civil Service were recruited for a decade. As Meta Zimmeck has pointed out, in 1921 and 1922 there was genuine fear of what might happen if ex-servicemen were not given preference, but by the late 1920s and 1930s there was no such obvious rationale for giving concessions to men at the expense of women.[28]

Male employers of female white-collar labour faced an additional problem, namely that it might happen either that well-educated women would apply directly for higher ranked posts, or that women from the clerical grades would be promoted. Faced with the possibility of working with women, employers did their best to prevent it. The boundary between public and private was always most tightly drawn around the professions and around political life. By confining women to strictly segregated employment as telegraphists, typists, shorthand writers and routine clerks, employers certainly sidestepped the resistance of male clerks and those unions who believed the best policy was to organise women,[29] but they also acted in accordance with the idea that fundamental sexual differences existed which made men and women suitable for different kinds of activities.

This rationale was made explicit by the various committees that passed judgement on the role of women in the civil service. Before the First World War, the MacDonnell Commission recommended that women should continue to be recruited on 'separate lines' because in 'powers of sustained work, in continuity of service, in adaptability to varying service conditions, the advantage lay with men'.[30] It was therefore in the interests of the state to confine them to the clerical work they could do well. When the Gladstone Committee examined the issue of women's employment in 1918, it also stressed that women and men did not have the same talents. The Report repeated frequently that women and men were not 'interchangeable': 'The evidence we have taken on the subject convinces us that, having regard to the existing differences in the opportunities of education and in the general mental equipment of young men and women, it would be unsafe to introduce women forthwith as interchangeable with men.'[31]

The Committee felt that it was generally agreed, for example, that 'women do not stand either a sudden or a prolonged strain so well as men'. Arguments based on sexual difference underpinned assertions that women had not performed as well as had popularly been claimed (chiefly in the press) during the War. In fact little hard evidence was produced on this score. After the War such evidence became increasingly difficult to find, because the standard of ex-servicemen recruits was so low. Committees relied primarily on what they felt to be the incontrovertible fact of sexual difference.

The Gladstone Committee invoked the classic distinction between mechanical or clerical and intellectual or administrative work, making it fit their view of male and female capacities and constructing a pyramid of grades wherein women were confined to the lowest clerical work.[32] The border between clerical and administrative grades was elaborately policed throughout the inter-war years by a series of formal and informal devices. When the civil service grading structure was reorganised in line with the National Whitley Council Report of 1920, the lowest clerical grade of writing assistant continued to be reserved for women while the middle clerical grades were assimilated to the detriment of women, whose grades moved down relatively; those of men moved up.[33] The division between mechanical and intellectual work was effectively maintained with special tests introduced for women seeking promotion. These, together with the marriage bar, which was rigidly enforced in most white-collar occupations during the inter-war years, ensured that very few women would rise within the system. The MacDonnell Commission had asserted in 1912 that 'the responsibilities of married life are normally incompatible with the devotion of a woman's whole time and unimpaired energy to the public service'.[34] Arguments resting on sexual difference and the separation of spheres were at their strongest when the possibility of women combining work and marriage was raised. The marriage bar was most effective in forestalling debate about women's promotion. As Cohn points out, the marriage bar was one of the most important devices employers used to ensure a female labour turnover that was beneficial in an occupation using tenure-based salary scales.[35] For the most part, the bar disappeared in the course of the First World War, but in the Post Office it was retained until 1963.[36]

Possibly as important as any factor in confining women to sexually segregated jobs was the informal work culture. The power of this has been recognised in Crompton and Jones' recent work on present day clerical workers. Only one of the three establishments they investigated practised overt discrimination of the sort that was common before the War, but the organisational culture of all the establishments served as an effective deterrent to women's advancement. Crompton and Jones also found the work culture to be the most important factor explaining the degree of female unionisation: where the subordinate position of women was most explicit, trade union organisation was weakest.[37] Informal methods of confining women to particular jobs are difficult to document in the present and well-nigh impossible for the past. Celia Davies' recent action research project to promote equal opportunities in the National Health Service (NHS) uncovered the workings of the 'golden pathway', whereby male workers are informally given the information and encouragement necessary to seek advancement and women are not.[38] In the case of clerical workers, this sort of mechanism must play a part in explaining Crompton and Jones' findings that while male clerical workers are promoted women are not. Certainly very few women have surmounted the obstacles to promotion within the civil service. Virginia Woolf remarked acidly of the fate of female examination candidates: '"Miss" transmits sex: and sex may carry with it an aroma'.[39] It was probably this elusive sense of the impossibility of women gaining advancement to the kind of work that men believed women were constitutionally incapable of that prompted Hilda Martindale to write: 'How were these services (of women) to be used in the future? The answer, as always, when women's work is under consideration, depends on how the man who has to make the decision estimates himself'.[40] Martindale served as both the Chief Woman Inspector of Factories and as Director of Women's Establishments in the Treasury and wrote a sympathetic but even-handed and reliable narrative history of women in the civil service, published in 1938. This is the only point at which she permits herself to speculate as to the mainsprings of male behaviour beyond the bounds delimited by the written evidence.

The employers view of women's proper place was for the most part shared by male clerks. A male clerk writing to the *Manchester Guardian* in 1886 complained of competition from both female and German clerks and wanted a clerks union in Manchester to control their entry. He also argued that if clerks were given better wages they would be in a position to keep a wife at home.[41] This argument, together with issues of the moral risk of men and women working together, were very similar to the concerns raised by skilled male manual workers at the end of the nineteenth century. The concept of a family wage which emerged in the later nineteenth century was fundamental to determining the mix of activities women engaged in, because its acceptance as an ideal ensured that women took primary responsibility for husband and family and that their paid work was regarded by society and by themselves to be of secondary importance. The ideal of a family wage was legitimised by ideas of masculinity and femininity. By the late nineteenth century the ability to 'keep' a wife was a measure of working-class male respectability. Geoffrey Crossick has described the insecurities of the lower middle class, whose numbers included the male clerk, and their desire to distinguish themselves from manual workers.[42] But Guy Routh's figures show that the earnings of male clerks and of skilled male manual workers were very similar on the eve of the First World War.[43] The male clerk thus felt doubly socially threatened, by the skilled male manual worker and by female (and foreign) competition.

As Wally Seccombe has pointed out, there were two possible arguments about the family wage, first if men were able to earn a family wage then wives could stay at home, and second, only if the employment of women were curtailed would men's wages rise.[44] On the whole, manual workers and their unions stressed the second of these and pressed for the exclusion of women. The weaker National Union of Clerks formally pursued a policy of equal treatment for male and female clerks, making it clear that its primary aim was to protect the position of the men:

The low status of the male clerk is due to the fact of the female clerk working for less wages than her competitor; therefore, whether the production of female labour be equal to male labour or not, to raise the salary of the male we must also raise the salary of the female and value her work as equal to that of the male. If the male clerk be so unwise as to be antagonistic to or ignore the female, he will make her his rival, and in time she would prove herself so powerful as to oust the male out of his position.[45]

In fact while the salary levels of male clerks remained comparable to those of skilled manual workers until the mid 1930s, after that they declined steeply. Given the relative weakness of their position, a high degree of sexual segregation with its concomitant lack of promotion opportunities for women was probably the best outcome that male clerks could have secured.

Women's view of clerical work

Fiona McNally has argued strongly that female orientations to work are not fixed solely by upbringing, education and domestic obligation, but are sustained, modified and frustrated by the experience of work itself.[46] In many respects, late nineteenth and early twentieth century women clerks shared men's views as to women's place and the sense of propriety to be observed when men and women worked in the same establishment. There was therefore very little opposition to sexually segregated employment, or to the marriage bar; not even strong feminists believed it possible to combine marriage, motherhood and paid work. On the whole, women expected to work until marriage; both Mostyn Bird and Barbara Hutchins felt that women's expectations of a 'Visionary Deliverer' in the form of a husband was responsible for their low level of job commitment.[47] But it is as likely that McNally is correct and that the characteristics of the jobs rather than the worker were to blame. Women expected and occupied lowly positions, which in turn helped determine their lower levels of trade union organisation and which served to reinforce their low pay and status. The pattern of cause and effect is therefore very difficult to unravel. While women clerks may broadly be seen to have accepted the nature and conditions of their work, which in turn made the role of housewife additionally attractive, oral evidence also indicates that many women clerks took pride in their work and women certainly sought greater financial rewards for it.[48] Women clerks firmly believed in the value of their work, but did not necessarily demand greater opportunities.

Clerical work was undoubtedly respectable and therefore had much to recommend it to women. Even the most poorly paid office work would be preferable to a factory job to a woman who valued her respectability, for most observers were agreed that factory girls were 'low types'.[49] For this reason, government offices were more prestigious places of employment than those in industry, the latter often being close to the plant.

Conditions in the lowest paid work could in fact be far from ideal. A 1901 Report on offices in London found that half of the fifty-five offices visited had no separate lavatory facilities for women.[50] For women workers anxious about respectability, strict discipline and sexually segregated employment were positive features. The work of the lowest grade of clerk might appear repetitive and onerous, yet oral evidence shows that considerable pride was often taken in, for example, keeping the best ledger.[51] Nor were the material rewards for the work great. Even women paid as little as £40 a year were still expected to manage to dress themselves like ladies. Women living at a distance from their workplace travelled in the cheaper workmen's trains before 8 am and spent the extra time in one of the new ABC or Lyons cafés.[52] Tea and buns tended to form a substantial part of the office worker's diet. Outside London, women clerks found their bootbill heavy because of the amount of walking they did. A dry year sometimes saved expense because they could use a bicycle.[53] The woman clerk who did not live at home was by far the worst off. In 1898 Clara Collet reckoned that such a woman might have to pay £40 for unfurnished lodgings.[54] It was, as women clerks themselves pointed out, therefore quite impossible for the woman earning between 14 and 30 shillings to live in comfort. They reported that of the three remaining housing options – the semi-charitable 'Home for Business Ladies', the furnished room without board or attendance and the third rate boarding house – most women were forced into the latter and even then had not money to spare for holidays or emergency medical expenses.[55] Despite their claims to respectability, a substantial number of women clerks struggled to survive on what social investigators calculated to be subsistence minimum wages.[56] It was perhaps not surprising that many seem to have looked forward to marriage and housekeeping. As one writer in *My Weekly* put it in 1920: 'Why every time I think of the little home Will and I are getting together, I know that I'll never want to type another word when I get scrubbing and cleaning and cooking in it'.[57]

Sidney Webb complained in 1891 that 'For women's work the "gentility" of the occupation is still accepted as part payment'.[58] Women clerical workers certainly accepted sexually segregated employment as fit and proper. However, they protested about their rates of pay, and overall discontent with the representation they received from the National Union of Clerks led in 1903 to the formation of the Association of Women Clerks and Secretaries. Women who remained single and in employment had particular cause for concern about pay.

Indeed for the inter-war period there is considerable evidence of bitterness among unmarried women workers, directed in the main against married women. For example, the National Spinsters Association, formed in 1935, believed that part of single women's pension contributions were going to support widows, who were able to draw pensions at fifty-five years.[59]

Women's expectations of their working lives were nevertheless relatively low. The range of occupations open to them was, as we have seen, small. The lowest grade clerical work demanded only an elementary school education. A slightly higher grade of work required a typing or shorthand course which might cost 3–5 guineas, while a full Pitman's course in shorthand typing, business methods, book-keeping, arithmetic and languages cost 30 guineas in 1905.[60] Such a course would be the province of largely lower middle and middle class girls. The highest grades of clerical work required a secondary education, but as late as the 1930s only 78 per cent of children aged eleven or over managed to get a free secondary school place and only 20 per cent went at all. The competition for free places was fierce and working class women's autobiographies often record either the disappointment of winning a place and then not being allowed to go, because of the family's poverty or because secondary education for girls was not felt to be appropriate, or the embarrassment occasioned by poverty if they did go.[61] Nevertheless, Kathleen Sanderson's oral history of the lives of some twelve women civil servants showed how the fortunate conjuncture of a free place in secondary school followed by high grade clerical employment in the civil service at a time (in the 1930s and 1940s) when the status of such work was still high among women, resulted in considerable social mobility, which they consolidated by marriage.[62] All these women looked back on their work with satisfaction and pride, and yet all who had married had both expected and been content to leave work when they did so.

Writing of women's work in agriculture in the eighteenth and early nineteenth centuries, Keith Snell has concluded that changes in the structure of the economy are sufficient to explain the changes in women's work.[63] Despite the necessarily circumstantial nature of much of the evidence discussed in this chapter, the example of clerical work in the late nineteenth and early twentieth centuries does not seem to support his conclusion. Rather, it would seem that the nature and conditions of women's clerical work should also be considered as part of the construction of masculinity and femininity. Male employers and workers had firm ideas as to women's proper place as wives and mothers. In the case of male workers in particular such ideas may be seen as entirely self-serving. But to count them merely as props legitimating a strategy designed to limit the opportunities of women workers is to risk underestimating the strength of the belief in 'natural' sexual difference, something that is essentially shared by modern theorists of women's employment when they resort to women's 'natural' role as childbearer and childrearer to explain women's position in the workforce. In large measure women did not question these beliefs and accepted the idea of 'a woman's job and a woman's rate', just as they accepted responsibility for home and family. But, they did not necessarily also accept the low value accorded their work – either in the workplace or at home.

Notes

1   M. Stacey, 'The division of labour revisited or overcoming the two Adams', in P. Abrams *et al.* (eds.), *Development and Diversity: British Sociology, 1950–1980*, London, Allen and Unwin, 1981, p. 14.

2   See, for example, Theodore W. Schultz, *The Economics of the Family: Marriage, Children and Human Capital*, Chicago, University of Chicago Press, 1974.

3   Jane Humphries, 'Class struggle and the persistence of the working class family', *Cambridge Journal of Economics*, 1, 1977.

4   R. D. Barron and G. M. Norris, 'Sexual divisions and the dual labour market', in D. Leonard Barker and Sheila Allen, *Dependency and Exploitation in Work and Marriage*, London, Longman, 1976.

5   Sylvia Walby, *Patriarchy at Work*, Oxford, Polity Press, 1986.

6   Michael Young and Peter Willmott, *The Symmetrical Family*, New York, Pantheon, 1973.

7   Trevor Lummis, 'The historical dimension of fatherhood. A case study', in McKee and M. O'Brien (eds.), *The Father Figure*, London, Tavistock, 1982; Elizabeth Roberts, 'Working wives and their families', in T. Barker and M. Drake (eds.), *Population and Society*, London, Batsford Academic Press, 1982; and A. Whitehead, 'Sexual antagonism in Herefordshire', in D. L. Barker and S. Allan (eds.), *Dependence and Exploitation in Work and Marriage*, London, Longman, 1976.

8   Martin Oppenheimer, *White Collar Politics*, New York, New York Monthly Review Press, 1985, p. 123, has suggested that employers today may face a similar tension between their 'patriarchal' desire to retain a personal secretary and implementing a more rational, cost-effective method of office organisation.

9   Walby, *Patriarchy at work*, p. 154.

10   Samuel Cohn, *The Process of Occupational Sex-Typing. The Renovation of Clerical Labor in Great Britain*, Philadelphia, Temple University Press, 1985.

11   Lee Holcombe, *Victorian Ladies at Work. Middle Class Working Women in England and Wales, 1850–1914*, Hamden, Conn., Archon Books, 1973, p. 216, Table 6f.

12   Meta Zimmeck, 'Strategies and strategems for the employment of women in the civil service', *Historical Journal*, 27, 1984, pp. 901–24.

13 Catherine Hakim, *Occupational Segregation*, Research Paper No. 9, London, Dept. of Employment, 1979.

14 Quoted by Linda Grant, 'Women's work and trade unionism in Liverpool, 1890–1914', *North West Labour History Society Bulletin*, no. 7, 1980–81, pp. 76–7.

15 Richard Hyman, 'Introduction', in Richard Hyman and Robert Price (eds.), *The New Working Class? White Collar Workers and their Organizations*, London, Macmillan, 1983, pp. 7–8 summarises the changing position of the male clerk.

16 Holcombe, *Victorian Ladies at Work*, p. 151.

17 Hilda Martindale, *Women Servants of the State, 1870–1938*, London, Allen and Unwin, 1938, p. 66.

18 This continues to be clearly demonstrated, for example, in relation to the computerisation of office work. Louise Kapp Howe, *Pink Collar Workers*, New York, G. P. Putnams, 1977, p. 169 has drawn on personal testimony to illustrate the effects of computerisation on the work of a female accounts clerk in the USA in the mid-1970s.

19 Gregory Anderson, *Victorian Clerks*, Manchester, Manchester University Press, 1976, p. 60.

20 Rosemary Crompton and Gareth Jones, *White Collar Proletariat: Deskilling and Gender in Clerical Work*, London, Macmillan, 1986.

21 Cohn, *Process of Occupational Sex-Typing*.

22 Martindale, *Women Servants of the State*, p. 18.

23 Olive Schreiner, *Woman and Labour*, London, Virago, 1978, p. 201, (first published 1911).

24 Elizabeth Fee, 'The sexual politics of Victorian anthropology', in Lois Banner and Mary Hartman (eds.), *Clio's Consciousness Raised*, New York, Harper Torchbooks, 1974.

25 Henry Maudsley, 'Sex in mind and in education', *Fortnightly Review*, XV (1874), p. 477.

26 Fee, 'The sexual politics of Victorian anthropology'.

27 Zimmeck, 'Strategies and stratagems'.

28 *Ibid.*

29 Walby, *Patriarchy at Work*, p. 154.

30 Quoted in the *Final Report* of the Treasury Committee on Civil Service Recruitment after the War, Cmd. 164, 1918, p. 6.

31 Cmd. 164, p. 7.

32 Meta Zimmeck, 'The Employment of Women in the British Civil Service, 1870–1939', forthcoming PhD dissertation, SUNY Stonybrook.

33 Zimmeck, 'Strategies and strategems'.

34 Quoted in Martindale, *Women Servants of the State*, p. 149.

35 Cohn, *Process of Occupational Sex-Typing*.

36 Walby, *Patriarchy at Work*, p. 240.

37 Crompton and Jones, *White Collar Proletariat*, pp. 189–91.

38 Celia Davies and Jane Rosser, *Processes of Discrimination: A Report on a Study of Women Working in the NHS*, London, DHSS, 1986.

39 Virginia Woolf, *Three Guineas*, London: Hogarth Press, 1938, p. 92.

40 Martindale, *Women Servants of the State*, p. 71.

41 Anderson, *Victorian Clerks*, p. 59.

42 Geoffrey Crossick, 'The emergence of the lower middle class in Britain: a discussion', in G. Crossick (eds.), *The Lower Middle Class in Britain, 1870–1914*, London, Croom Helm, 1977.

43 Guy Routh, *Occupation and Pay in Great Britain 1906–79*, London, Macmillan, 1980, p. 124.

44 Wally Seccombe, 'Patriachy stabilized: the construction of the male breadwinner wage norm in nineteenth-century Britain', *Social History* 11, January 1986, pp. 53–76.

45 Quoted by Grant, 'Women's work and trade unionism in Liverpool'.

46 Fiona McNally, *Women for Hire. A Study of the Female Office Worker*, London, Macmillan, 1979.

47 M. Mostyn Bird, *Women at Work*, London, Chapman Hall, 1911, p. 3 and B. L. Hutchins, *Women in Modern Industry*, London, G. Bell, 1915, p. 13.

48 Meta Zimmeck, 'Jobs for the girls: the expansion of clerical work for women, 1850–1914', in Angela V. John (ed.), *Unequal Opportunities: Women's Employment in England, 1800–1918*, Oxford, Blackwell, 1986, p. 166, stresses this point and cites the example of best qualified women clerks leaving the civil service at the turn of the century to seek better wages in business firms.

49 For example, the comments of Clara Collet in Charles Booth, *London Life and Labour*, Vol. IV, p. 313.

50 Anderson, *Victorian Clerks*, p. 17.

51 Kay Sanderson, ' "A pension to look forward to . . . ?" Women civil servant clerks in London, 1925–1939', in Leonore Davidoff and Belinda Westover (eds.), *Our Work, Our Lives, Our Words*, pp. 145–60.

52 Teresa Davy, 'Female Shorthand Typists and Typists, 1900–39', unpublished MA thesis, University of Essex, 1980, p. 80.

53 Clara E. Collet, *Educated Working Women*, (London, P. S. King, 1902), p. 86.

54 *Ibid.*, p. 74.

55 Martindale, *Women Servants of the State*, pp. 164-5.

56 Set at £1 a week by B. Seebohm Rowntree in 1914 (*The Human Needs of Labour*, London, Thomas Nelson, 1918, p. 117).

57 Quoted by Davy, 'Female shorthand typists and typists', p. 87.

58 Sidney Webb, 'The alleged differences in the wages paid to men and to women for similar work', *Economic Journal*, December 1891, pp. 635-62.

59 *Report* of the Committee on Pensions for Unmarried Women, Cmd. 5991, 1938, p. 39.

60 Teresa Davy, ' "A cissy job for men; a nice job for girls": women shorthand typists in London, 1900–1939', in Davidoff and Westover (eds.), *Our Work, Our Lives, Our Words*, pp. 124–44.

61 John Burnett, *Destiny Obscure: Autobiographies of Childhood, Education and Family, from the 1820s to the 1920s*, London, Allen Lane, 1982.

62 Sanderson, 'Social mobility in the life of some women clerical workers'.

63 Keith Snell, 'Agricultural seasonal unemployment, the standard of living and women's work in the South and East, 1690–1868', *Economic History Review* XXXIV (1981).

3 Susanne Dohrn

Pioneers in a dead-end profession:
the first women clerks in banks
and insurance companies

Janet Hogarth was an ambitious woman, not easily satisfied with the meagre job prospects open to middle class women at the end of the nineteenth century. An Oxford graduate in Philosophy, German and Greek, she became the first woman clerk to be appointed by the Bank of England in 1893. In her autobiography, *Recollected in Tranquility* published in 1936, she painted a dismal picture of women's clerical work at the turn of the century:

I say unhesitatingly that clerical work for women thirty years ago, when I was first adventuring into the business world, was a soul destroying avocation, from which any woman, let alone a woman of higher education, might well prey to be delivered.... Most of it was deadly dull and not too handsomely rewarded.[1]

Why was women's clerical work so boring and so badly paid? The example of banks, insurance companies, shipping firms and big merchant houses shows how, beginning in the 1870s, companies used the abundant supply of unemployed young middle-class women to reorganise their expanding work load to cut down their salary expenses. The women of course were only too happy to be offered respectable jobs which on the surface didn't seem to be too badly paid. Only later they realised that their work was cut off from the ordinary business of the companies and that they weren't offered the career opportunities open to men.

Little is known about privately employed women clerks before the First World War. We known that their numbers increased dramatically in the last thirty years of the nineteenth century, as shown in table 3.1.

Table 3.1 *Women commercial clerks, England and Wales 1861–1911*

1861	1871	1881	1891	1901	1911
274	1,412	5,989	17,859	55,784	117,057

Sources: *Census of England and Wales*, 1861, II/III, p. XXXII; 1871, III, pp. 14, 19; 1911, Preliminary Report, Table 64, p. 263.

Who were these women? Which companies employed them? What work did they do? The search for source material proved to be disheartening. Companies hardly ever kept their staff records. Only a few insurance companies and banks, mostly located in London, were able to provide helpful details about numbers of women employed, salaries paid and rules of conduct. The reasons for hiring these women can only

be glimpsed: from newspaper articles, clerical magazines, autobiographies, handbooks on business management and the occasional
notes found in the minutes of boardroom meetings.

Together with information on the declining job prospects of men
clerks, the beginnings of women's work and its reasons emerge.
Companies, confronted with growing expenditure for their ever
increasing clerical labour force began to subdivide the work. Menial
and repetitive tasks, formerly done by male apprentices, were given to
women. For the men these tasks had been the first step on the escalator
to success. For the women they became the beginning and the end at
the same time. Both the companies and the male employees profited
from this; hiring an increasing number of low paid women for menial
work saved expenses and kept the male clerks in good mood because
the more interesting and better paid work became their exclusive
domain.

In order to understand women's position in the clerical labour
market it is necessary to look more closely at what happened to their
male counterparts, because the changes which happened to men clerks
in the second part of the nineteenth century prepared the ground for
the employment of women. I will then deal with the women clerks:
their pay, their working conditions, how they were selected by the
companies and how the companies justified their employment. Taken
together this information makes clear why women's clerical work far
from improving the economic and social position of women became an
avocation which only reinforced their dependence on men.

When James McBey stepped into the world of a mid-Victorian
banking house, his new job gave him the feeling of belonging to the
better strata of society: 'My new toggery lay on the chest beside my
bed. The long trousers were the symbol of manhood; the hard black
hat, the dickey and cuffs were the livery of respectability.'[2] James
McBey's pride reflected his privileged position. As a banking clerk he
belonged to the most respected and best paid branch of the clerical
profession. Besides and even more important he had joined the Bank at
a most favourable time. Around the middle of the century business was
expanding rapidly and young men who joined the clerical profession
could be sure to move up to responsible positions rapidly.[3]

Twenty years later the situation had changed. Starting in the 1870s
pamphlets, newspaper articles and booklets were published in which
clerks voiced their discontent. 'All the lofty aspirations and hopes of

youthful days have remained unfulfilled; and he who was looking forward to independence finds himself, at the close of his career, worse off than at the outset.'[4] Thus the London 'City Clerks' complained in 1880. Not only was clerical work badly paid but it had become a low status job, as Benjamin Guiness Orchard, the founder of the Liverpool Clerks' Association pointed out in 1870: '. . . however intelligent and estimable a man may be . . . if someone but whispers "he is only a clerk!" at once he is at a discount, and almost anybody takes precedence of him.'[5]

Of course the discontented clerks were quick to point out the culprits. First of all, the young and 'uneducated' clerks were blamed who had more and more filled their ranks and, by their cheap competition, had lowered the wages. 'The supply exceeds the demand, and the natural consequence is that all those who have no other means must offer themselves at almost any price . . .',[6] the city clerks wrote. A solution to this problem was offered by the *Clerk's Journal* in 1888: '. . . young men whose only prospect is to take their places in the lower ranks of clerks must be crushed out of existence.'[7]

Not only young male competitors were blamed for low wages and the decline in job prospects. From the 1870s onwards women, though still few in numbers, had to take a fair share of male hostility. 'The new rivals are all the more formidable', the 'city clerks' wrote, 'as they can take low wages, are fair accountants, docile at the desk, and at least as accurate in copying as men are.' Of course the 'city clerks' knew where these women really belonged: 'Whilst women now enter into competition with men on the field of mental labour, . . . they omit to learn how to mend a stocking or to cook a steak.'[8]

Such attacks on women clerks were completely out of proportion. In 1880 women clerks made up only 3·3 per cent of all commercial clerks employed in England and Wales.[9] However much these women were blamed, they could not have caused the decline in job prospects, wages and status of the profession. Neither were the young and so called uneducated clerks to blame for that matter. Young men and women had only answered a newly developed demand in the clerical labour market – the demand for cheap labour.

Behind this discontent lay severe changes in the organisation of the clerical labour force. For a long time clerks had been promoted according to seniority, not only seniority of age but seniority of the time spent in the service of the company.[10] It is well documented for the banking business, but salary lists of insurance companies and other

businesses suggest similar practices.[11] The reasoning behind this is
obvious: clerks who knew that their wages would steadily rise and
provide them and their families with financial security saw no reason to
deceive their employers. 'The greatest stimulus to improvement in the
clerks is an impartial system of promotion', wrote James William
Gilbart in his *Principles of Banking* in 1882. This was particularly true of
banks because their risk was greater than that of other companies. So
Gilbart's advice to bankers was to 'err (if he errs at all) on the side of
liberality.'[12] For the clerks of the Bank of England before the turn of
the century this meant that by the time they were forty-one years old
they would earn at least £280 per annum, whatever their merits.[13]

Do your work patiently and wait for your chance to come was the
advice of many a writer of business manuals. They all took for granted
that success would eventually come. In a book *To Young Men Going Out
Into Life* published in 1891 the readers were told that

there is seldom a man in office or warehouse to whom opportunity does not come. A
sudden vacancy occurs through sickness or accident in the position just above yours.
Who is to fill it? Yourself, probably, if by your previous attention to your duties you have
won esteem, and are trusted by those above you. Only a temporary promotion, perhaps,
but if you discharge your duties well, permanent promotion is certain to follow.[14]

Reuben Spencer's words reflect some of the changes which had
happened between the 1850s and the 1890s. The almost automatic
promotion which was implied in the system of seniority had been
discarded by many companies. The reason: it had become too
expensive. As companies grew, more and more clerks were needed to
cope with the increasing paperwork. Not all of them after a certain
number of years could be offered supervisory jobs. Besides which it
wasn't necessary to pay high salaries to men doing only menial work.
The result was widespread discontent. Something had to be done to
keep male clerks in good humour.

The employment of women was seen as a way out, in particular by
big companies. It served two aims at the same time. First of all it saved
money, because women workers were traditionally cheaper than men.
This was also true for middle-class women, who were looking for work
in steadily increasing numbers. Secondly women employees could be
kept separate from the men. Etiquette and modesty demanded this,
and many big companies prided themselves in the efficiency with
which it was achieved. At the same time, keeping women in separate
departments made it easier for the company to keep them at menial
work. As long as it was impossible for women to even go so far as to look

at the men's work it was out of the question to apply for these jobs. By keeping the women to low paid and menial jobs the system of seniority could be kept up for the men clerks. Thus men profited too from the employment of women.

One of the first records we have about women clerks we owe to Arthur J. Munby's interest in exotic women's occupations. One night in April 1864 when he went dancing in Soho he met a young lady. She had arrived 'straight from business', as she told him. This immediately aroused Munby's interest, as he hadn't heard of anything like that before. He asked her to dance, bought her drinks and of course questioned her. What he found out was worth his time and money. He had discovered a rarity. Munby wrote in his diary: '. . . she was a merchant's clerk! A bona fide female 'city clerk': a copying clerk in fact in a mercantile house in Old Broad Street.'[15] She was twenty-two years of age and had already worked for the company for three years, when she met Munby. She knew three or four other companies in London, which employed women clerks as well.

The conditions under which these women worked were rather atypical for the time as we will later see. Munby writes:

the male and female clerks sit together in a large room. For herself, she sits on a high stool, at a desk, with the others, copying invoice letters or whatnot, all day: 'our sleeves get worn with leaning on the desk, and our white cuffs get dreadfully inked', says she. The male clerks are pleasant companions enough; but there is no flirting: 'when you're all in business to-gether, it's different; and besides, we've no time.'[16]

The young lady knew that she had obtained the job primarily because she earned less than her male colleagues. She proudly told Munby that the firm liked the ladies best, for they did the work as well as the gentlemen, and were paid less. They received between 20 and 30 shillings per week, and worked eight hours a day, from 9 to 5, from 10 to 6, or from 12 to 8, according to circumstances.[17]

These women clerks enjoyed a sense of freedom which was unknown to other women of their class. Under the pretext of having to work late, they went dancing, without their parents knowing about it:

'I tell my father that I've been kept at work at the office: and then he says what a shame it is to keep girls working till such hours, and why don't they put men clerks to it? So they do, I tell him. But my mother suspects that I cant (*sic*) be at business till eleven o'clock at night . . .'[18]

In Munby's diary there are only faint hints as to the social background of these first women clerks. They probably came from middle-class

families, without having fallen victim to the superficial and soul-
destroying education that was offered to girls of that class in the
nineteenth century. Munby, who wasn't too keen on middle-class
women for that very reason, liked her the better for it. He commented:
'. . . she had none of the frippery and giggling frivolity of other girls of
her class', but to the contrary, 'she looked a most queenly self-reliant
young woman, able to make her way in the world, and neither diffident
nor over-bold.'[19]

From later sources we know that companes paid great attention to
the social background of their women clerks. Their selection followed a
similar pattern as that for the men clerks. Qualifications were
important but so was the right family background. Relatives of men
already on the staff were preferred. This is reflected by a letter of
application written to Baring Brothers, merchant bankers in 1900. 'I
believe you employ ladies as clerks in some departments of your office
& I write to enquire whether there is any chance of an outsider (i.e. a
lady unconnected with any of your Staff) getting on the list, provided
qualifications & references are satisfactory.'[20] Unfortunately the
Honourable F. H. Baring's answer to this request is unknown.
Sometimes these job applications read like a family pedigree. 'I am
twenty-two years of age', Dorothy Blake wrote in 1903. 'My father was
Mr. E. T. Blake, and my maternal grandfather Mr. C. W. Turner both
late partners of the firm of Messrs. Burne Turner and Co. . . .; my
paternal grandfather was rector Bramerton, Norfolk.' After that she
proceeds to name her typewriting speed and job experience.[21]

We don't know how these women fared with Baring Brothers, but
we do know what the Prudential Insurance Company in London
expected of its future employees. 'They must all be the daughters of
professional men', it said in 1890 in *The Office*, a magazine for men and
women clerks. Miss Hanslip, one of the first women to be employed,
was the daughter of one of the company's main shareholders.[22] The
Bank of England selected her women clerks according to the same
criteria as her men clerks: three-quarters of them were to be nominated
by the Directors, one-quarter was to be chosen from the daughters of
clerks. One in every twenty-one was to be nominated by the Governor.
Additionally the women had to pass a medical examination by the
company physician.[23]

Little is known about the process of decision making within
companies preceding the decision to employ women. The Bank of
England is one of the few to have kept a detailed account of this.

Therefore I will deal with it in a more detailed way. Before the Bank of England embarked on the dangerous experiment of employing women, the Directors contacted other institutions which already had some experience with this novelty. First of all the Postmaster General was asked if he could recommend a suitable lady. It seems that he couldn't because the Bank then turned to the Royal Commission of Labour, which happened to be the only Government institution to have women university graduates on its staff. After much consideration, the Directors chose two women clerks who had worked for the Royal Commission: Miss Janet Hogarth and Miss Elsee. Miss Elsee was twenty-two, educated at Girton College in Cambridge and had graduated with honours in the History Tripos in 1892. Janet Hogarth was twenty-seven years old, had studied Greek, German and Philosophy at Lady Margaret Hall in Oxford and graduated with first class honours in Philosophy in 1888. She spoke German as well as French and had worked as a Philosophy teacher at the Cheltenham Ladies College before she obtained a post with the Royal Commission where she was entrusted with the general supervision of the women clerks.[24]

When Janet Hogarth was offered work with the Bank she was intrigued. Quite rightly she had the feeling of belonging to the elected few. After all, clerks of the Bank of England were at the very top of the clerical labour force.[25] Janet Hogarth remarked '. . . women in ordinary banks were unheard of, and their introduction into the Bank of England, of all places, caused a mild sensation.'[26] Unfortunately for Janet Hogarth and her colleague Miss Elsee, the Bank didn't trust the intellectual abilities of its high class university graduates. The women were given returned bank notes to count and sort, work which had formerly been done by young apprentice clerks or uncovenanted clerks. Janet Hogarth commented:

it was almost unbelievably soothing to sit in the quiet upper room with . . . nothing to do but lay out banknotes in patterns like Patience cards, learning all about the little marks on them, crossing them up in piles like card-houses, sorting them in sixties and finally entering their numbers in beautiful ledgers made of the very best paper, as if intended to last out all ages.[27]

The two women were given six months to learn the new job. Of course they had mastered it in six weeks, as Janet Hogarth said, 'but it wouldn't have done to hurry the Bank – the very suggestion smacked or irreverence . . .'[28]

The work Janet Hogarth and Miss Elsee were given reflects the lack of job opportunities for educated women in the nineteenth century.

Teaching or clerical work for many years were almost the only alternatives. The number of applications for the first four posts at the Bank in 1894 shows the incredible demand for work experienced by women. Nearly 500 women applied, only 30 of these were known to the Directors, 20 were the daughters of clerks employed by the Bank and the rest were 'general applications'.[29]

These women didn't necessarily go into clerical work because they liked it but rather because there wasn't anything else to do. 'Whether I liked it or not, I had to go to work', a women who had started as a typist at Cassells in London in 1906 told me. Another woman, interviewed by Anna Davin, described the choice between becoming a teacher or a typist. Her brother encouraged her to go into teaching, but that meant three years as a pupil teacher and two years at college which would cost him far too much money she thought. When he asked her what she would like to do she told him about the girls in the Yost typewriting showroom in Holborn and that she would like to learn typewriting like those girls in the Yost Typewriter Office.[30] A few years later none of the glamour which had attracted this woman was left. Winifred Eastment, born in 1899, describes her attitude to a career as nebulous and indecisive apart from one thing. 'Perversely, I only knew beyond a shadow of doubt what I did *not* want to do, and that was to slog in a city office', she wrote in her autobiography.[31]

The job obviously didn't prove what it had promised, not for women clerks in banks and insurance companies and not for women shorthand typists. Why this was so will be shown in the next section.

With reference to the lady clerks, they would not in any way prevent a fair development of male clerks. There had been an unusually large number of male clerks appointed last year, and the lady clerks were doing a class of work that they could not get satisfactorily done by the male clerks.[32]

With these words Mr Harden, the Director of the Prudential Assurance Company in London, in 1874 tried to dispel the shareholders' doubts concerning the employment of women. Obviously he was successful because the number of women steadily increased from 50 in 1974 to 250 in 1891 and almost 300 in 1894.[33] They were exclusively employed on clerical work of a routine character; copying letters, filling in forms and schedules. This they did better and more rapidly than men, Sidney Webb was assured, when he investigated the differences of wages paid to men and women in 1891.

Table 3.2 *Salaries of women clerks at the Prudential Insurance Company, London (£)*

Age	17–25	On interims 2nd year	3rd year	On promotion	17 heads of division	1 Matron
	32	42	52	60	95	115

Source: Sidney Webb, 'The alleged differences in the wages paid to men and women for similar work', *Economic Journal*, I, 1981, p. 653.

(To compare this with men's wages; a boy clerk, starting at the Prudential at the age of fifteen, was paid £20 per annum. At the age of eighteen he earned £50, at twenty-one years he earned £150.[34])

In 1888 the *Liverpool Clerk's Journal* indicated that more and more women were doing simple clerical work; 'Insurance companies discovered that such work as copying out policies could be done almost, if not quite, as well by girls as by men, and what is still more important in these days of small dividends, at a considerable reduction of costs.'[35]

The Prudential wasn't the only insurance company to employ women. The London, Edinburgh and Glasgow, the Pearl in London and the Refuge in Manchester did so as well. All these companies were specialised in 'industrial insurance'. This probably wasn't a co-incidence. Industrial insurance was labour intensive: It gave life cover for weekly payments and was therefore specially adapted to the needs of working-class people. Having to deal with small and numerous sums, industrial insurance companies were forced to economise earlier than others.

Little is known about the work conditions and pay of these first women clerks. At the London, Edinburgh and Glasgow, which was taken over by the Pearl in 1910, the women had to fill in sixty policies per minute. They were paid 8s 4d per week, that is £22 per annum. Like the women at the Prudential, they worked Mondays to Fridays from 10 to 5 and Saturdays from 9 to 1. They had half an hour's break for lunch which was provided by the Pearl.[36]

Unlike the woman interviewed by Arthur J. Munby, the women working for insurance companies had no chance to meet their male colleagues. Women entered and left the building through a separate entrance and worked different hours. This was true for the Prudential and the Pearl. A former Pearl employee (male) remembers '[The Ladies Office] with its own private entrance . . . was presided over by the intimidating Mrs Cook, who kept her charges strictly apart from the male clerks and even discouraged the departmental head, Mr Young, from entering on her preserve.'[37]

The work these women did wasn't as light as men tried to make the world believe. 'It was hard going in those days', remembers Florence Walker, who had started to work for the London, Edinburgh and Glasgow in 1904. Like their male colleagues the women had to work at high desks and sit on uncomfortable stools. To ensure a rate of sixty policies per hour strict discipline was enforced. The supervisor and her assistant were 'terrors' Florence Walker recollects. They would stand at the foot of the marble staircase leading to the exit at 4.55 p.m. in order to catch any staff leaving early. Those who came late in the morning were fined sixpence out of a weekly wage of 8*s* 4*d*. After five years of service the women were entitled to two weeks of annual holidays.[38]

Working conditions at the Prudential were somewhat better. A report in *The Office* from 1890 gives details:

The women worked in three rooms, 300 feet long, lined with white tiles and provided with ample light by means of large windows. They sat on cane seated chairs facing each other over low mahogany desks. They were given an hour for lunch, which was served in a luncheon room on the 4th floor. A library with over 300 volumes provided them with reading material. If they chose not to exert their minds but breathe some fresh air instead they could promenade on the roof. Their working hours were from 9 to 5.[39]

This strict division of male and female clerks was the rule. When the Sun Insurance in Leeds in 1895 hired its first 'Lady Typewriter', she was well guarded from the curiosity of her male colleagues. In a letter to the head office in London, the Leeds branch manager reassured his worried superior: 'Miss Bentley our Lady typewriter at present occupies the typewriter desk in the general office. It is perfectly screened from public view and most convenient for the proper carrying out of her work.' He was thinking though of installing her and her typewriter in the basement, because 'the latter is very light, sunny and dry and quite suitable for the purpose.'[40]

In the 1870s, not only insurance companies but banks started to employ women clerks. Baring Brothers and Rothschilds were the first. The women worked in the coupon departments checking coupons that had been presented for payment and entering them into ledgers. When dividends were due for collection they had to cut the coupons from the Bond or certificate.[41] Nothing is known about the women working for Rothschilds but there is some information on those employed by

Barings. They earned £39 per annum, that amounts to a weekly wage of 15 shillings. The supervisor of the 'ladies department' was paid £65. In comparison, in 1875 none of the fifty-five male clerks earned less than £80, their average salary was £330.[42]

Contrary to the men, the women did not receive regular increases. In 1879, when the first two women left the Bank after six years of service, they still earned £39. Like the men, they had to serve a twelve month probation period before they were taken on staff. They weren't entitled to a pension. The consequences this had for the women is shown by a letter Gertrud Middleton wrote to the Honorable F. H. Baring in 1895. She had joined the company in March 1875 at an annual wage of £39, and was financially destitute when she had to leave for health reasons.

I left the service of Messrs Barings Bros. . . . through failure of sight after 20 years of work and I write to ask your kind consideration of the same. It has been impossible to save anything the first 9 years only receiving 15/- a week but since that time have been gradually raised to 30/-. I am no longer young and shall find great difficulty in keeping myself, and I trust you will be good enough to grant me some remuneration.[43]

There is no hint that her plea has been granted. The first woman clerk to be granted a pension had joined Barings in 1886 for an annual salary of £45. When she had to leave twenty years later for health reasons she was paid a pension of £65.[44]

Only in 1919 the 'Regulations Relating to Pensions' were passed. They applied to members of the permanent staff and messengers who had worked at least ten years for Barings and had to leave for health reasons or because they had reached the retirement age which was fixed at sixty-five for men clerks and messengers and sixty for women clerks. The amount depended on the years of service. It started at ten/sixtieths of the last annual wage and went up to forty/sixtieths after forty years of service. Women who left the company because they got married were given a marriage bonus of £5 or £10 according to their years of service.[45] The hours were the same as in insurance companies: from 10.00 to 5.00 with an hour for lunch. From 1901 onwards they were granted twenty-four days of annual holidays.[46]

Discipline at Barings was at least as strict as at the Pearl. The 'Regulations for the Coupon Department' from 1901 enforced complete silence. 'During business hours the rooms are to be kept as quiet as possible and no general conversation is allowed', it said in the regulations. Even during the lunch break women had to refrain from discussing 'undesirable subjects' such as religious matters. Women whose work was finished or who had nothing to do for the time being, were permitted to read, write or do needlework. This sounds very liberal but has to be compared with what was allowed to men clerks. They used to retire to the adjoining pubs until they were ordered back to the office. As with the Pearl and the Prudential, the division of the sexes was strictly enforced; 'Members of the General Office Staff are not to go into the (Coupon S. D.) Department except as required by the business and are not to remain there unnecessarily.'[47]

Baring's and Rothschild's experiment was obviously carried out in secrecy because the Bank of England claims to have been the first Bank in London to employ women. In fact, they started twenty years later, in 1893. Fortunately in this case we know some of the reasons which led to the employment of women and the difficulties which beset it. When the decision to employ women was made, the Bank had difficulties of making ends meet. The Government had squeezed it, interests were low. Senior officials were therefore charged with the search for economies in administration. The search proved to be successful. It was discovered that certain tasks could be done more cheaply by women.[48]

Conditions for the women clerks were somewhat better than in other companies. They got a free meal and twenty-seven days of annual leave. After ten years of service they were entitled to a pension if they had to retire for health reasons or because they had reached the age of fifty. For the numerous women who didn't get married this meant that they could look forward to old age without having to face financial disaster. Out of the eighty-nine women, having been taken on by the Bank between 1894 and 1907, fifty-nine were still in the service of the Bank in 1907. Thirty had left, most of them to get married. At least one of them – Janet Hogarth – had left, because she found the work too boring.[49]

The Bank went out of its way in order keep the women separate from the men. Men clerks who would have liked to set their eyes on their new colleagues were disappointed. A former bank employee complained in his autobiography:

The streets, it was held, were safe enough, but once she (the woman clerk S. D.) entered this forbidding fortress every imaginable horror was predicted. Exalted personages bent their great intellects to the problem of mitigating the frightful perils. First, they had to devise a way to and from the women's watertight quarters where they would not even catch a glimpse of a male, and the first rule was that from this new nunnery they should under no circumstances whatsoever, enter another office . . . It was pointed out to them that behind the closed doors opening on to the passages lurked horrible males with hairy goat legs to pounce on them as they passed.[50]

The women weren't only kept apart for morality's sake. Rather it may be argued that a strict division of labour was easier to enforce if it went with different accommodation for men and women.

First of all, the women found temporary accommodation in the Sub-Cashier's room whose office was divided in two by means of a wooden screen. Thus all contact between male and female clerks was prevented. In the long run this wouldn't do. To provide adequate accommodation for the forty women to be employed from August 1894 onwards, a whole new department was built. The women had to wait until the First World War before they were allowed to move freely in the Bank.[51]

In April 1894, salaries and increases for women clerks were laid down by the bank.

Table 3.3 *Salaries of women clerks at the Bank of England (£)*

	Present salary	Annual increase	Maximum wage
Miss Hogarth	157·1	10·10	210
Miss Elsee	105	7·10	157·10
Two assistants	73·10	5·5	105
Sorters	54·12	3·18	85·16

Source: Bank of England, Women Clerks, –. 4. 1895, E 4/1.

With a salary of more than £150 Janet Hogarth probably was one of the best paid women in London. Even the £80 earned by women sorters after only four years of service could be regarded as a good wage. This view was not shared by Janet Hogarth though. She wrote:

Thirty shillings after several years' experience was considered a good rate of pay. Yet, allowing for her expenses in fares and food out, it barely sufficed to keep a girl of good middle-class origin and decent standard of living in one of the smaller hostels or boarding houses. Hardly any of these asked less for room and 'partial board' than 25 shillings. Nothing to speak of was left for clothes, less than nothing for recreation. In fact, though it might mean comfortable pocket-money for daughters living at home, even when they contributed to home expenses, it was bare subsistence and nothing more to a girl on her own.[52]

Women's wages were to become a point of discussion in the later history of the Ladies Department.

The employment of women wasn't supported by all of the male staff. In particular the Chief Accountant, a Mr Stuchbury, was a formidable opponent. He and the Chief Cashier were two of the most important officials of the Bank whose word wasn't easily overheard. In November 1895 Mr Stuchbury sent a report to the Secretary of the Bank in which he summed up his experience with the Ladies Department. Taken as a whole the report was unfavourable. This is all the more surprising because Mr Stuchbury deliberately admitted that the conduct of the women clerks had been very satisfactory and that they had done their work well. Comparing their work to that of the Uncovenanted Clerks, whom they had partially superseded, it appeared that the women had succeeded in getting as much or even more work done than their male colleagues. Stuchbury wrote: 'The women work much more steadily and quietly than the youths, and may perhaps be expected to get through more work in the course of the year.'[53] Indeed thirty-seven women counted as many bank notes as forty-seven men had formerly done. Besides, the women made fewer mistakes.[54]

In Mr Stuchbury's eyes these advantages did not outweigh the potential disadvantages: '. . . the youths have more energy and endurance, and can, it is thought, be relied on to respond more effectively to the pressure of a very heavy day's work.' Additionally women were absent more often than young male clerks. Their rate was 1·75 per cent compared to 1·6 per cent of the men's! Besides women were allowed twenty-seven days of annual leave whereas Uncovenanted Clerks were only entitled to twelve days. All this the Chief Accountant might have been able to accept had there not been the women's high wages. According to him the women earned on average £10 more than the young men formerly employed on the work. Therefore he drew the conclusion that it would be best to abolish the Ladies Department once and for all and return to an all male staff.[55]

By accident Janet Hogarth got wind of the affair and succeeded in warding off this attack. The Secretary's remarks on the Chief Accountant's memorandum explain why the Bank decided to stick to the women's department:

[The Secretary] sees the force of the Chief Accountant's argument, so far as it regards the initial increase in cost to the Bank . . . [but] supposing other and more general employment can be found for the women clerks, a considerable future saving of expense should be effected when it is borne in mind that, according to present scales of salary the majority of Women Clerks would not attain higher pay than £85 against £300 eventually earned by all other clerks who remain in the service till they reach the age of 45 years.[56]

In fact the Bank of England and other companies had worked out a dual system; men were offered upward career mobility and its concomitant, steadily rising salaries; women were offered comparatively higher starting salaries and hardly any upward mobility. Keeping women in Ladies Departments reinforced this dual system. In a report by the Bank of England from March 1921 this was explicitly stated. The sexes were segregated, it said, because women should not see and perhaps envy the more interesting work the men were doing.[57]

Envy or not, it turned out that the women in the Ladies Department of the Bank of England weren't happy with their work. But instead of openly giving vent to their feelings, they got ill. In March 1903 out of sixty-three women fifteen suffered from writer's cramp. From this Bank officials drew the conclusion that women were more susceptible to nervous disorders. The Chief Accountant, Mr Stuchbury, therefore suggested a much more careful selection of candidates and an immediate dismissal should the illness be discovered. Additionally he commended a lowering of the age limit from eighteen to twenty-five down to seventeen to twenty. Stuchbury remarked '. . . a nervous breakdown during the first few years of service, and it is within that period that it usually occurs, if at all, should be treated as disqualifying a Clerk for her position. Roughly speaking a woman under twenty-five can adopt another career.'[58]

This time the Bank investigated the matter carefully. A Commission was set up to examine the question of women clerks. It came to the conclusion that the nervous disorders were not due to any innate weakness of the female sex but to the monotony of their work. In the words of the commission; '. . . it was felt that women could hardly be expected to spend a life-time's service sorting Notes.'[59] Whereas young men were never expected to do this work for more than two years, the women were offered nothing else for their whole working lives. In her autobiography Janet Hogarth severely criticised this:

what is the outlook for the bright intelligent girl brought in to do permanently the routine work formerly left to boys just leaving school? Many institutions – the Bank of England for instance – have made this experiment. For a time it works well. The girls show a zeal and zest which no boy thinks of emulating. But the trouble comes when they grow to be middle-aged women and are still kept at work only fit for beginners. They have become mere machines. Their task does not occupy their minds even while they are at it. They can . . . still think their own thoughts, very depressing thoughts when the future offers nothing but a delusive pension twenty or thirty years on, with little energy left to enjoy it when it comes.[60]

Janet Hogarth acted accordingly. She left the Bank in 1906, because her chances of advancement were too limited for her ambitions: 'Had I been a man, I might have aspired to the glories of Chief Accountancy or Chief Cashiership. As a woman, I could only look to security, consideration and a pension.'[61] Why was Janet Hogarth the only woman who left to find another job? The reason is simple enough. Not having had a university education like her, most women clerks had no alternative. The number of suitable jobs for middle-class women being limited, their only choice was to exchange one badly paid position for another equally badly paid one. Besides they only knew too well that they owed their employment to their low salaries. In the face of widespread antagonism against women's employment in the nineteenth century, they can't be blamed.

Notes

1 Janet Hogarth, *Recollected in Tranquillity*, London, 1926, p. 138–9.

2 James McBey, *The Early Life of James McBey 1883–1911*, Nicholas Barker (ed.), Oxford, 1977, p. 24.

3 Benjamin Guiness Orchard, *The Clerks of Liverpool*, Liverpool, 1871, pp. 21, 46; R. H. Mottram, *Bowler Hat: A Last Glance at Old Country Banking*, London, 1940, p. 25.

4 *The City Clerks: The Difficulty of their position and its causes . . . By one of them*, London, 1870, p. 1.

5 Orchard, *The Clerks*, p. 7–8.

6 *The City Clerks*, p. 28.

7 *The Clerk's Journal*, I, 1 Sept. 1888, p. 2.

8 *The City Clerks*, p. 34–5.

9 *Census of England and Wales*, 1911, Preliminary Report, Table 64, p. 263.

10 Gregory Anderson, *Victorian Clerks*, Manchester, 1976, p. 30–1.

11 For examples see Susanne Dohrn, *Die Entstehung weiblicher Büroarbeit in England 1860 bis 1914*, Frankfurt am Main, 1986, p. 225–30.

12 James William Gilbart, *The History, Principles, and Practice of Banking*, A. S. Mitchie (ed.), London, 1882, p. 13.

13 Bank of England, Memorandum Respecting the Salaries etc. of Clerks, 12 May 1874, File E 4/5.

14 Reuben Spencer, *To Young Men Going Out Into Life*, London, 1891, p. 5.

15 Derek Hudson, *Munby, Man of Two Worlds: The Life and Diaries of Arthur J. Munby*, London, 1972, p. 156.

16 *Ibid.*

17 *Ibid.*

18 *Ibid.*, p. 157.

19 *Ibid.*, p. 156–7.

20 Baring Brothers, File HC 1.14.4.48.

21 Baring Brothers, File Dep. 86.1.

22 'The lady clerk in clover', by Woman, in *The Office*, III, 3 May, 1890, p. 9; R. W. Barnard, *A Century of Service: The Story of the Prudential 1848–1948*, London, 1948, p. 28.

23 Bank of England, 'Women clerks', –. 4. 1895, File E 4/1.

24 Bank of England, 'Character of Miss Hogarth and Elsee', 26.10.1893, File E 4/1.

25 Mottram, *Bowler Hat*, p. 34.

26 Hogarth, *Recollections*, p. 153.

27 *Ibid.*, p. 155.

28 *Ibid.*, p. 155–6.

29 Bank of England, 'Women clerks', 4.4.1894, File E 4/1.

30 Interview of Susanne Dohrn with Mrs Morgan, born 1890, in London 1984; Interview of Anna Davin with Mrs Bartholomew, born 1882, from Poplar 1973.

31 Winifred Eastment, *We Weave as We Go*, London, 1972, p. 75–6.

32 *The Post Magazine*, XXXV, 1874, p. 109.

33 Sidney Webb, 'The alleged differences in the wages paid to men and women for similar work', *Economic Journal*, I, p. 652–3; Mrs. H. Coleman Davidson, *What Our Daughters Can Do for Themselves*, London, 1894, p. 26.

34 Margaret Mulvihill, 'The White Bloused Revolution: Privately Employed Clerks in London 1890–1914', unpublished MA Thesis, Birkbeck College, London, 1981, p. 18.

35 *The Clerk's Journal*, I, 1 Oct. 1888, p. 11.

36 Florence Walker's Recollections of Office Life, Pearl Archives.

37 John Williams, 'More Than We Promise: A Century of the Pearl Assurance Company', unpublished Pearl History, Pearl Assurance Company Archives, London, 1962, p. 158.

38 Interview by Susanne Dohrn with Florence Walker of Worthing, former Pearl employee, 1984.

39 *The Office*, 3 May 1890, III, p. 9.

40 Guildhall (London) MS 18 263, II, p. 198.

41 Written Communication with Dr. John Orbell, Archivist, Baring Brothers London, 23 May 1984.

42 Baring Brothers, File HC 1. 14. 1. 12,; Counting House Expenses and Clerk's Salaries List. (No file no.)

43 Baring Brothers, File HC 1. 14. 3. 68.

44 Baring Brothers, File HC 1. 14. 1. 12.

45 Baring Brothers, Regulations Relating to Pensions, File Dep. 86.1.

46 Baring Brothers, Regulations: Coupon Department, File Dep. 86. 1.

47 *Ibid.*; Joseph Wechsberg, *Hochfinanz International*, München, 1966, p. 153.

48 R. S. Sayers, *The Bank of England 1891–1944*, II, Cambridge, 1976, pp. 607, 614.

49 Clara E. Collet, 'Salaries and Conditions of Employment of Women of 18 Years and Upwards as Typists in April 1907', Public Records Office (P.R.O.) London, T 1 10 146/5925, p. 10ff.

50 H. G. De Fraine, *Servant of This House: Life in the Bank of England*, London, 1960, p. 118.

51 Bank of England, 'Memorandum on the Temporary Accommodation of Women Clerks', 8. 1.1894, File E 4/1; Hogarth, *Recollected*, p. 164.

52 Hogarth, *Recollected*, p. 147/8.

53 Bank of England, 'The Employment of Women Clerks in the Bank of England', Chief Accountant's Memorandum, 29.11.1895, File E 4/1.

54 Sayers, *The Bank*, p. 615.

55 Bank of England, Chief Accountant's Memorandum.

56 Bank of England, The Secretary's Remarks upon the Chief Accountant's Memorandum, Jan. 1896, File E 4/1.

57 Sayers, *The Bank*, p. 617.

58 Bank of England, Employment of Women Clerks, Chief Accountant's Report, 23.3.1903, File E 4/1.

59 Bank of England, The Committee Appointed by the Court of the 19th March Last, to consider the Question of Women Clerks, Report to the Court of Directors, 10.11.1903, File E 4/1.

60 Hogarth, *Recollections*, p. 148–9.

61 *Ibid.*, p. 168.

4 Gladys Carnaffan

Commercial education and the female office worker

'The most valuable kind of commercial education is that which a man gets and can only get in an actual business house'.[1]

The above commonly held attitude as expressed by Michael Sadler, MA, Professor of the History and Administration of Education, Manchester University, epitomised the problem that beset commercial education. Fifty years earlier, T. H. Green, Philosopher and Lecturer of ancient and modern history at Balliol College, who as Assistant Commissioner for the Schools Inquiry Commission, visited King Edward V School in Birmingham reported that

When one course of study is taken by all the boys of promise, the other by the backward boys, who don't profess to aim at the higher education, the latter inevitably becomes a secondary care to the masters. If the majority of the upper boys, on the other hand, or the more promising of them, lapse from the higher to the commercial studies the standard of the school, as a place of classical education for the few, inevitably falls.[2]

In the space of half a century, nothing had changed. The objection to the teaching of commercial subjects was that it had always been considered by a certain section of the population to be something inferior – a second class type of education.

In spite of this view, commercial education had not been altogether devoid of advocates, for Philip Magnus had long since been pointing out that 'nowhere was the creative spirit more lacking than in the education for commerce'.[3] Lord Rosebery, MP, at the opening of the Keighley Institute in 1887, also stated that 'another objection which is constantly raised, is that our merchants or their agents are deficient in a modern commercial training'. To bring home this point he referred to Germany's success, stressing that 'She did not make education more abstract, but more practical, more technical, more commercial, and she has made herself by that great effort, long preserved in, the most practical people I think on the face of the globe'.[4]

In fact Prussian schools had been giving practical studies since 1806, and the Continental countries generally had had education systems which catered to meet their commercial internal and external needs. Whilst primarily they were established to withstand the severe competition of English industry, they also supplied personnel efficiently and adequately trained to their newly established industry and commerce. The attitude held in these European countries was voiced by a director of an academy in Vienna when he stated that such commercial training was aimed 'not only at training the minds of the pupils but also at forming their character'.[5] Quite a submission when compared to the general attitude held by many educationalists in this country'.

Why the neglect?

Tradition upheld the resourceful amateur; a man learnt on-the-job and passed on his knowledge verbally. This was the situation all the way from the boardroom to the workbench. But during this same period, the European countries and America were creating institutions for technical and commercial education that could turn out 'educated practical men'.[6] Why then was British industry and commerce still reliant on the 'amateur'?

Whilst reform and expansion had been taking place in the Victorian public schools, these had been inspired by the religious and moral idealism of the Romantic Movement, and had ignored the realities of the industrialised world.[7] The gulf that existed between industry and such education, between the 'practical' man, despising education on the one hand and the public schools on the other, concentrating on the classics, religion and games, remained as wide as ever.[8] It would be wrong to suppose that there was general hostility to giving any education at all to the working classes, but it was certainly believed that only a very elementary kind of education should be made available to them. Lord Armstrong, a leading North East industrialist, spoke for many when he said, 'the most the average man required was a grasp of the three 'R's' and discipline!'[9]

A widespread middle-class belief was that too much education would make the working classes discontent with their lot, which would lead to insubordination and political unrest. But these were the days when Britain justly laid claim to the title 'Workshop of the World'. The Great Exhibition of 1851 had upheld this, with Britain winning nearly all the scientific and industrial awards but by 1867, at the Paris Exhibition, it was a different story. Britain secured less than one in ten awards. An awareness of this situation had long been shown by Lyon Playfair, Professor of Chemistry at Edinburgh University in 1858, and other technical education lobbyists. Later, Reports on Technical Education of 1867–68 confirmed that Prussia, Belgium, France and the U.S. were way ahead. Britain at that time had no institution worthy of comparison, for example, with the Paris School of Commerce which was founded in 1820, the Superior Institute of Commerce in Antwerp or America's chain of thirty commercial colleges. In fact, there was nothing in this country to compare with what was happening abroad.

Whilst technical education reached a peak in the 1880s with the setting up of the Royal Commission on Technical Education in 1884, and the foundation of the National Association for the promotion of Technical and Secondary Education in 1886, commercial education still lagged behind. In an address entitled 'Commercial Education' in 1888 to the members of the Glasgow Local Association of the Educational Institute of Scotland, W. G. Blackie, Ex-Lord Dean of Guild, started by stating that

Until quite recently no-one would have thought of preferring such a request to anyone; for the simple reason that no-one took any special interest in the education of those who were destined to be engaged in commercial pursuits – the most numerous, as well as most important, classes of the community – that to which is entrusted the carrying on of the commerce of this great empire.[10]

Neglect was still being voiced after the turn of the century when in 1911 the Director of the School of Commerce in the University of Liverpool was re-emphasising the plight of commercial education. He declared that

England has contrived for a long time to undertake a very respectable share of this planet's commerce without any system of commercial instruction worth mentioning and has also contrived to lose a great deal of what it formerly did and is in a fair way to lose a great deal more through default of appropriate education.[11]

The various Commissions reiterated the problem constantly and laid forth what was happening abroad Prominent men were in accord on the same issue, but in spite of the alarm that was being sounded, the imbalance of the situation begs the question as to why should an equally important element in the expansion of trade and commerce be so repeatedly ignored?

In seeking a possible solution to this, it is useful to look at the definition of the term 'technical education'. Whilst few historians make a clear distinction, Hall suggests it means 'vocational education of the working classes generally'.[12] This definition may be considered all the more appropriate in its inclusion of commercial education in light of the reports that followed the Great Exhibition. For example the Taunton Report of 1868[13] whilst identifying the wishes of parents for their children's education, did so by suggesting a division by grades. Those children who were to stay at school until eighteen or nineteen years of age, would go to first grade schools; those leaving at sixteen years to second grade schools; and those leaving at fourteen years to third grade schools. Within the Report's terms of reference the second grade schools were to offer 'a certain amount of thorough knowledge of those subjects which can be turned to practical use in business'. The third grade, the report stressed, 'belongs to a class distinctly lower in the scale' and goes on to what was termed 'a clerk's education'. This type of education was seen as strictly a means to an end, and with the labelling of second and third grade, it is little wonder that commercial education was looked upon as an inferior type of education. The Aberdare Report, 1881, turned out to be the most far-sighted in its recommendations for the commercial subjects mentioned therein became the basis of many courses in the teaching of office workers over the ensuing years.[14]

Later Commissions emphasised the need for commercial education but always under the technical education umbrella. The passing of the Technical Instruction Act 1889 and the allocation of the revenue through the Local Taxation (Customs and Excise) Act 1890 for Technical Education again showed that the arguments of the pressure groups for technical education were being upheld. An awareness of what would happen was shown by Mr Howard Vincent, MP for Sheffield Central, at a meeting of the Committee for Education on 6th August 1887, when he asked

If the definition of the Technical Instruction Bill is clearly understood to embrace commercial instruction; and if it will be undoubtedly open to Local Authorities to provide educational facilities under the provisions of the Bill for the study of foreign languages, commercial correspondence, advanced book-keeping, the principles of banking, exchange, discount, customs and mercantile law, and to obtain grants for proficiency in such subjects, as knowledge of handicrafts and sciences of local trades?[15]

The reply that the intention was to give freedom to localities as to choice of curriculum, subject to the approval of the Science and Art Department, meant that the local authorities were to be given no clear guidance from the Government and any decision made by them required the sanction of the Science and Art Department which was principally engrossed in the promotion and development of technical and art subjects. It would seem that again the urgency for commercial education was to be overlooked. As was to be expected, response to the Acts varied from area to area, as those responsible for implementing them conceived that function, which invariably meant technical education at the expense of commercial education.

It is a complex picture which shows that perhaps what commercial education lacked was a lobby to parallel that of technical education. Whilst references do occur within the various Acts[16] it would appear that the exponents of technical education were not sufficiently aware of the need for office or management training. In fact, there were signs of movement against office work, for it was stressed at the first reading in the House of Commons of the Technical Instruction Bill, July 1887, that the 'main purpose was to provide opportunities for the great centres of industry to develop technical education. One aim was to turn people away from clerical occupations and into industrial ones'.[17] Paradoxically, in spite of what appears to be gross neglect on the national front of what constitutes an important element in the education of a large proportion of the workforce of this country, initiatives were to come from a variety of sources.

Meeting the needs of commercial education

In view of its standing in the world of education and society generally, it is hardly surprising that pressure for commercial education was meagre and failed to meet needs. The result of this laissez-faire approach meant that initially it was left to the private establishments to cater for the increasing demand for commercial subjects. Dalvi argues that this had two very unfortunate consequences. First the standards of instruction were poor in both quality and effectiveness, and secondly instruction was in the hands of people who possessed no adequate knowledge or experience. But he also suggests that such attempts, however inadequate, saved commercial education from extinction.[18] The Rev. Dr. C. Badham, Headmaster of Birmingham and Edgbaston Proprietory School (who, therefore, had his own axe to grind), was less charitable to the private commercial school. His address at the prize-giving in September 1864 attacked both the grammar school for its shortcomings and the private school for their spacious claims of providing a commercial education, stressing 'No parent . . . would be satisfied with the wretched mechanical acquirements which are now the common results of five or six years at a commercial academy'.[19] Nevertheless, it was left to the private schools to cater for popular demand by providing what was necessary. Dr Arnold, writing in 1832, had thus described the commercial or English schools at which a considerable proportion of the sons of tradesmen and farmers received their education – 'the subjects were obviously geared up to their intended business in life, e.g. he learns Land Surveying if he is to be brought up to agricultural pursuits, or book-keeping if he is intended for trade'.[20]

Although such schools frequently came under attack, it would appear that they were more receptive to new ideas and more ready to experiment than the old endowed grammar schools. Such was their contribution that subsequent reforms in the curriculum can be largely traced to their influence and it was through the efforts of these private agencies that the main impetus gathered force. Whilst it is difficult to assess the amount of private provision available, for teachers held classes in their own front rooms, hired rooms, church halls or established schools of varying sizes, it can certainly be said that their numbers were on the increase. This situation was typical throughout the country but an interesting example of what was not typical, from the point of view of size and efficiency, was an organisation which was to stretch from Scotland to the North, West and East of England. It started as a small training centre in Edinburgh in 1878 by George Skerry, a Civil Servant, who saw the need to prepare candidates for the new Civil Service examinations, resulting from the findings of the Royal Commission 1875,[21] whereby entry to the Civil Service, Post Office or Customs and Excise, was to be by competitive examinations.

Examinations had become the recognised legitimate means for achieving control of entry to the various commercial professions since the early part of the century, and the Civil Service, as one of the major employers of clerical workers, demanded candidates for such work to produce either a certificate of general education or to sit a special examination.[22] Such was the response to Skerry's initiative that similar facilities were provided in Glasgow, which eventually became the main centre. The second remarkable move on the part of George Skerry was the provision of correspondence tuition, another 'first' in the country. This Correspondence College, started in 1880, formed an integral part of Skerry's expanding empire and played a vital role in supplementing and cementing what was offered in the day and evening classes. Eventually a chain of colleges was developed, mainly by the efforts of George Stewart who joined George Skerry in 1885 and who eventually became principal and proprietor, stretching from Glasgow and Edinburgh to Dundee, Newcastle and Liverpool, thus catering for an area the whole of Scotland, North, East, West and the Midlands of England.[23] These colleges, along with the development of the Correspondence College, created an extension to the country as a whole, as well as overseas, which was to last until the latter part of the twentieth century. Whilst the chief goal of the colleges in Scotland had been preparation for Scottish Universities and Profesional Preliminary examinations, as well as commercial work, the main emphasis of the English colleges lay within the sphere of commercial and office training courses, with some preparatory and grammar school work alongside.

Skerry's statistics show the number of successes gained in one year had risen from thirty in 1878–79 to 4,188 in 1957–58. The accumulated total in eighty years shows 301,597 successes. A breakdown of this figure is as follows:

61,689 passes in the various university and professional preliminaries
32,747 successes in Civil Service competitions for appointments in government offices
202,211 Office Training certificates
2,757 medals[24]

In view of this success, Skerrys must be acknowledged as having made a major contribution to commercial education, following through its educational objective beyond into the realms of the work situation.

Outside such private establishments provision for the office worker, such as it was, came through on two main fronts. First, through the local chambers of commerce and mechanics' institutes, then later under the auspices of the School Boards' Higher Grade Schools. A division of opinion exists as to the success or otherwise of the mechanics' institutes but J. W. Godwin in his assessment of the Bradford MI in 1859, stated that 'next to Sunday schools, they have been one of the strongest powers in the wake of popular education, hitherto the greatest work of the 19th century'.[25] Others argued that 'lectures too often had an aimless sequence and many of the subjects were purely recreational'. Certainly evidence shows that by 1849, out of 204 mechanics' institutes in England and Wales, only 43 were mainly supported by operatives and mechancis.[26] Nevertheless, support did come through significantly from the lower middle-class which included mainly clerks and shop assistants. Although the move from a works situation to an office situation was recognised as a means of promotion, the office worker did not receive support for his education in keeping with those in the workshops. It could be taken that the very existence of this situation was the reason why the mechanics' institutes were inundated with clerical workers.

It would be wrong to suggest that the agencies looked at were the only means of provision for commercial education, but it was not until the latter part of the century that the first attempt outside the voluntary evening classes came with the establishment of the Higher Grade Schools. Throughout the country, these Higher Grade Schools proved to be attractive to both parents and pupils alike with their vocationally structured curriculum. An example of this popularity is seen when looking at the North East, an area at the forefront in providing these schools – Gateshead in 1885, South Shields in 1886 and Jarrow in 1887. By 1898 the Gateshead School Board was considering a proposal to use part of the Higher Grade School to provide commercial courses specifically for those who had passed the VII standard[27], whilst since 1886 the St John's Higher Grade School in nearby South Shields, had been open with the stated objective 'to provide a school, which, whilst maintaining active efficiency in the ordinary subjects, would also furnish for boys a thorough commercial or scientific education, and for girls a sound course of education and accomplishment'.[28]

By 1905 St John's was a distinctly commercial school, entrance to which was obtained through the Borough's Scholarships and Entrance Examinations. In addition to the usual subjects were taught short-hand, typewriting, book-keeping, commercial correspondence and office routine; this time for both boys and girls.[29]

In Scotland too, the Higher Grade Schools were immediately popular, being introduced to meet the needs of students who were prepared to continue their full-time education for at least three years before entering industrial or commercial pursuits. In accord with the English schools, the special function of these schools was to continue the instruction given in the primary schools. At the outset they were of two types – the Higher Grade (Science) School, and the Higher Grade (Commercial) School, according to the predominant feature of the curriculum. In two aspects were the Scottish Higher Grade Schools to differ from their English counterparts, first in that they presented pupils in the leaving certificate examinations, then later they were allowed to carry pupils till seventeen or eighteen years of age, permitting these pupils during their last two to three years to specialise along certain lines – literary, scientific, technical or commercial.[30]

It would seem that provision for commercial education was finally being structured through these Higher Grade Schools, but this was not to be the case. Certainly in Scotland there were few districts without such a school, and in a short space of time they were actually to outnumber the secondary schools by four to one.[31] However, within four years the Higher Grade Schools were to become virtually secondary schools and in their place supplementary courses were offered with a vocational bias to children over twelve years.

In England, ad hoc arrangements varied from region to region depending upon the School Board's views. For example, in the North East – despite evidence gained from the reports of the various school boards in the area which emphasised that their Higher Grade Schools were popular, 'doing good work without practically entailing any charge upon the rates for their maintenance', and in spite of a Report of the Royal Commissioners on Higher Elementary Schools[32] which stated that they were of the opinion that it was very desirable that a Higher Grade or Intermediate School be established in Newcastle, the 'capital' of the area – Higher Grade Schools were not developed in Newcastle. Evidence suggests that here again was a situation whereby commercial education was overlooked in preference to technical education. Even though the demand was clearly there as shown by the numbers who passed through the School Board's evening classes.

Table 4.1   *Number of individual students attending the Board's Evening Continuation Schools and Commercial Classes*

Age	1896	1897	1898	1899
Under 14	61,196	86,877	19,402	66,414
14–18	163,643	186,435	220,462	275,622
18–21	38,070	43,484	48,536	64,501
Over 21	35,815	41,832	47,110	68,026
Total	298,724	358,628	435,600	474,563

Source: *Newcastle School Board Triennial Reports, 1898–1903.*

The demand was further emphasised when noting the provision made through Skerry's college in that city. Figures published on the closure of that College in 1968 showed that in Newcastle alone an estimated 50,000 secretaries, clerks, book-keepers, shorthand-typists and Civil Servants had received training there. By 1907 criticism was being voiced in Scotland too, resulting from the Report on Secondary Education of that year which seemed to suggest that moves were being made to discourage pupils away from commercial education subjects.

Whilst stressing that there was a need for pupils to stay on at school after fourteen years for 'they cannot possibly be expected to have received anything that is worth calling a commercial education at an earlier age', the point was made that the raising of the age without its natural concomitant – a satisfactory commercial curriculum – was to say the least, premature.[33]

An overall view shows a most unsettled profile of mixed provision but one of which the office worker was eager to take advantage. Whilst competitive examinations had become the accepted means of selection for a wide variety of occupations, it was conceivable that those outside these realms would look for a means of legitimising their multi-variable positions, positions which sometimes lacked definition, for it is not sufficient to state that a clerk or office worker is a person who carries out clerical duties in an office. A writer in *The Clerk* suggested 'A better definition of a clerk would be . . . the man left over after everybody's occupation had been defined, the man who did all the remaining miscellaneous work, and who very often did the real work for which a figurehead of assured position and handsome salary got the credit'.[34]

The saviour of these office workers was again to come from private initiative in the form of the Society of Arts (Royal after 1908), founded a century earlier by a body of public spirited men who joined forces to promote what they deemed to be the needs of society. As organisers of the Great Exhibition of 1851, and with their involvement in later exhibitions, they were aware of the advance of the continental countries not only in the technical but also in the commercial field. Recognising the void for office workers, they initially liaised with the mechanics' institutes and set up their first examination in 1856.[35]

Table 4.2 *Royal Society of Arts examinations, 1900–30*

| | Papers worked | | | |
	1900	*1914*	*1930*	*1985/86*
Shorthand	2,293	7,815	17,229	51,378
Typewriting	673	2,806	11,372	297,128
Book-keeping	3,684	11,883	25,385	8,934
Other commercial subjects	2,264	12,918	34,014	111,589
	8,914	35,422	88,000	469,029

Sources: *Half a Century*, Pitman 1932, p. 139; Royal Society of Arts *Report on Single Subject Examinations*, 1985/86, pp. 120–2.

Other contributors were to follow in the form of local examination bodies, or private college certificates, as awarded by Skerry's and Pitmans of London but the Royal Society of Arts' figures show consistent growth to this present day.

The significance of the RSA's success seems to have been overlooked by some historians. For example, Montgomery talks about 'limited success' and suggests that RSA examinations were 'tolerated'. Roach, on the other hand, whilst admitting that the RSA were 'doing useful work', went on to suggest that they 'lacked prestige necessary for real initiative', whilst Lockwood ignored its contributions altogether.[36] But the figures above cannot be dismissed as limited. A more crucial point is to note that, contrary to the norm of the times, the RSA's doors had always been open to women. Women speakers were encouraged and a committee was set up to promote better education for girls of all classes. It has been said that whilst the pioneering middle-class woman gave the female office worker her first assertively dignified step, the opportunities for the 'board-school' girl came when it became easier for her to acquire a commercial education.[37] The significance of the RSA examinations, which still predominate to this very day, played no small part in the process.

The female outlet

The two over-riding factors that were conducive to helping women in their demand for improved education, were the ever-increasing numbers of excess women, and at the same time, the growing demands of an industrial society for an expanding 'cheap' workforce. As more women became educated, so their demand that the professions be open to them grew. The Census Report of 1871 stated that 'They are excluded wholly or in great part from the Church, the Law and Medicine. Whether they should be rigidly excluded from these professions or be allowed – on the principle of freedom of trade – to compete with men, is one of the questions of the day'.[38]

But with such barriers in force 'women's work' came to connote work which required neither manual strength nor prolonged training. Along with the other socially acceptable middle-class occupations, clerical work was to provide a significant opening.[39] Conditions in the office world were all the more conducive to the employment of women by the other 'revolution' that occurred, namely, the introduction of the typewriter and telephone. These two inventions probably did more than anything else to create acceptable jobs for women outside the home. Such were the impact and implications for women that Christopher L. Sholes, who was responsible for producing the first popular typewriter, has been quoted as saying 'I do feel that I have done something for the women who have always had to work so hard. This typewriter will enable them more easily to earn a living. Whatever I may have felt in the early days of the value of the typewriter, it is obviously a blessing to mankind and especially to womankind'.[40] It would seem that from the first the typewriter was intended to be used by women in an office situation, an area which had been taboo to them previously.

It is interesting to note that the transfer of the telegraph offices in the 1870s to the Post Office which led to considerable expansion and reorganisation invariably created an increase in the number of clerks required. This increase proportionally was in favour of female employees.[41] Davin suggests that the extension of female employment was probably due to the enthusiasm of Frank Scudamore, who was in charge of the reorganisation. In his submission of the report, he argued the case in support of increasing female employees stressing that women's dexterity made them particularly skilled manipulators; that they took more kindly than the male employees to routine work, and bore long confinement with more patience; that they were cheaper ('the wages which will draw female operators from a superior class'); that being thus superior they were likely to write and spell better, and to raise the tone of the whole staff; that they were less disposed than men to combine for the purpose of extorting higher wages; and finally that there would always be fewer of them on the pension list because those who married would be likely to retire.[42] But Gertrude Tuckwell in 1912 maintained that 'the argument that girls are better workers is merely in the nature of an excuse and that cheap labour is the real object'.

The effect of the female impact resulted in an everlasting structural change in the clerical market which led Holcombe in 1973 to write, 'Since women represent the great majority of clerical workers in Britain today, it is simple truth that middle-class working women, albeit unorganised and underpaid still, are absolutely indispensable to the country's economy'.[43]

Status and qualifications

The question of economy and status seemed to dominate the whole position of female recruitment. The Prudential Assurance Company, for example, accepted only the daughters of professional men.[44] Because insurance was a predominantly male domain, the Prudential showed itself to be rather adventurous in employing women in 1872, although records show that as early as 1855 one of the Inspectors had appointed a few female canvassers. By 1890 they had 200 female clerks engaged in copying and writing letters, which confirms the advice given in early occupational manuals, which stressed good handwriting as the essential qualification with typing as a novel but by no means universally demanded extra; 'It is not so absolutely necessary for an English *lady* secretary . . . to know typewriting, but a knowledge of it, and also shorthand is of very great help in obtaining such a post'.[45] The predominant qualification required was that of 'social' background plus an average level of education.[46]

The Bank of England followed suit in 1894 by employing twenty-five female clerks. Although the Bank's candidates had to be nominated by one of the directors, this in itself was not enough. By insisting on an entrance examination, unless they had passed the Oxford or Cambridge local examinations, this in effect excluded the working-class and lower-class girls altogether, but as the need for more female office workers developed, it was recognised that class alone was not a sufficient qualification. For the working-class girls, the Education Act of 1870 opened the gates on to the work market but the division between status and qualification was to remain for some considerable time. In the North East, a region of male-dominant heavy industry, the shipbuilding firm of Wigham Richardson in 1886 thought themselves 'daring' in employing women in their offices and no qualifications other than that of 'status' was required.[47] Whilst nearby Clark Chapmans, who had been employing women in their draughting offices from 1882, a venture which had proved so successful, introduced lady clerks into their commercial department. Here qualifications were thought necessary in the form of a willingness to learn shorthand.[48]

The demand for qualifications other than status fell in line with the advent of what became known as the 'twin' arts, that is the development of shorthand and typewriting. The development of shorthand is well known, but its early gender link may not have been so obvious due to the later take-over by women. The initial situation was pointed out by a Miss Reynolds, at the reading of a paper entitled 'Shorthand for Ladies' at the public conference held in the Mayor's Parlour at the Manchester Town Hall in connection with the celebration of the Jubilee of Phonography and the Tercentenary of Modern Shorthand, on 29 August 1887, when she stated that 'until recently the art (shorthand) has been exclusively confined to men and practised by them; women have passed it by unnoticed, as having no reference to themselves and being entirely unfeminine'.[49]

Indeed, amongst the more famous male shorthand writers of the day was A. J. Sylvester, who was Parliamentary Secretary to Lloyd George from 1921–1923, as well as holding other outstanding positions.[50] Much earlier, George Birkbeck (1773–1841), founder of the mechanics' institutes, was reported to have taken down addresses in shorthand, 'a somewhat unusual accomplishment' at that period.[51] Generally the use of shorthand had been recognised by employers to be of utmost importance. This was emphasised by a Manchester businessman speaking to a group of young clerks, when he stated that he depended upon a good shorthand writer as much as he depended upon a good book-keeper.[52]

With the advent of the typewriter, the use of the 'twin arts' was ideal for correspondence. Some men saw the acquisition of these skills as being the instruments for the upgrading of their positions in what was fast becoming a declining market.[53] Thus it would appear that whilst typewriting particularly was gender-free in the beginning, it quickly became feminised for the term 'female typewriter' was the label borne by the operator of that machine. The time was propitious for the commercialisation of 'a machine to supersede the pen'. Not only had the volume of communication within and between companies grown, but the speed under which business transactions had to be carried out had increased. By 1882 Remingtons, already well-known as manufacturers of small arms and sewing machines, set up an international selling agency for the Sholes' practicable typewriter.[54] It has been suggested that as a result of marketing techniques, typewriting firms stimulated interest by having a lady operator demonstrating the machine's uses, at the same time likening it to the class-specific accomplishment of piano-playing. Anna Davin suggests, very plausibly, that it may have been the very revolution in such marketing techniques (the growth of advertising, publicity stunts etc.) which in part generated the need for more clerical workers, that gave women this break:

Rival firms each had their own model and organised lectures and exhibitions to publicise their wares, at which interest in the novelty would be further stimulated by having a lady operator demonstrate its paces . . . to convince the cautious of the machine's uses it (the typewriter company) would also supply machine and operator on a temporary basis by the day, or week, or longer. In this way, with the typewriter as Trojan horse, many a city sanctum was invaded by females, and the normal system of controlling entrance to clerical posts by advertisements, interviews and references was completely by-passed.[55]

The link between the typewriter and the female was established. The invasion was underway, for the importance of acquiring short-hand as well as typewriting was continually stressed in advice to would-be clerks: 'Typewriting and shorthand are twin arts, and young ladies who aspire to succeed in one of them, must make themselves proficient in the other. A typist who cannot write shorthand is very much like a pianist who cannot read music'.[56]

Between 1861 and 1911 the numbers of male office workers increased five-fold, whilst the numbers of women office workers increased no less than five hundred times over.[57] With this increase came the subsequent demand for training, and to meet this need, classes and schools sprang up throughout the country. In London alone, schools published in Pitman's Year Book rose from twelve in 1892 to thirty-nine in 1899. In the North, Skerry's Newcastle branch, as one of the larger establishments, ran a regular advertisement in the *Newcastle Weekly Chronicle*[58] which read:

'Few realise that Situations with salaries £70–£350 are
obtainable by simple ability to pass exams.'
APPOINTMENTS IN GOVERNMENT OFFICES
Male and Female
Enrol now for special preparation
SKERRY'S COLLEGE
Day, Evening and Postal Tuition
Successful students number over 6,000

Boy Clerks	age limits 15 to 18
2nd division clerks	age limits 17 to 20
Female telegraph clerks	age limits 15 to 18
Asst. Surveyor of Taxes	age limits 19 to 22
Lady Clerks, GPO	age limits 18 to 20
Assts. of Customs	age limits 18 to 21
Assts. of Excise	age limits 19 to 22
Male Telegraph Clerks	age limits 16 to 18

Success came in the form of certificates, often guaranteed on payment of a fee in advance, sometimes issued by the individual college or by the larger organisations such as the Royal Society of Arts or Pitmans. Certificates became a marketable force and the widest field of employment in which they were marketable was office work.[59]

In the closing decades of the nineteenth century there were – on a number of fronts (technical, commercial and financial) within the private as well as public sectors – both strong pressures and new opportunities making for large-scale enterprise.[60] This growth led to an ever-widening diversity of occupations for the office worker. Each particular business or trade required office workers specialised in that particular field. This specialisation in itself led to problems when considering forms of training or apprenticeships for the office workers.

The development of large-scale organisations such as the Civil Service and the railways led to a breakdown of what had once been a paternalistic relationship between the office worker and the employer. Employers now did not believe they had any responsibility towards their office staff, a view not held by their foreign competitors.[61] Unlike the trade apprentice, who at the end of an allotted time, emerged as a joiner or engineer, the entrant seeking a business or commercial career had no such opportunities for learning his job. There was no recognised 'ladder of promotion'.[62]

Whilst the workers in the banking and insurance offices had security plus the opportunities to advance their career education, which was being advocated and encouraged through their own particular association, those outside these groups had to seek their own route. Their problems were firstly that they possessed no common knowledge beyond the rudimentary skill of literacy and numeracy, the nature of commercial practice differing from one firm or industry to another, and secondly they were not bound as most professional groups by a code of ethics which specified their obligation to their clients or the public at large. Also they did not stand as many professional groups did, above the struggle for income. It was against this background therefore that many office workers turned to commercial education as a solution to maintain and improve their increasingly vulnerable position.

Competitive examinations had already become the generally accepted means of selection for a wide variety of occupations. Educational certificates thus became a legitimation for occupation and social status, and as such were increasingly valued as a means of individual social mobility. The general feeling was emphasised by

J. S. Mill in his statement that 'throwing open the Civil Service to competition was one of the greatest improvements in public affairs ever proposed by a government'.[63] The attraction of a commercial career was manifold; the comparative ease of entry, the prospect of rapid promotion and the assured respectability of the office worker over the tradesman or artisan. As the numbers of literate workers increased, so too did commercial education become more widely available through a variety of sources. These efforts were eagerly encouraged by the office workers own initiative. It was at this level that the Royal Society of Arts recognised the need and developed a system of commercial examinations that became nationally accepted and held in high esteem.

The expansion of general education, linked with the opportunity now afforded by following some form of commercial education, became the means of opening doors to both the male and female office worker but the result was an overstocked clerical market. What had previously been 'status' employment for the male clerk now became a low-level situation which led to the maxim 'once a clerk, always a clerk'.[64] The paternalistic system which had often guaranteed security and advancement had gone. For the female office worker the story was different. Office work had offered a means of escape for the educated middle-class and working-class female alike, but for different reasons. Initially for the former it was regarded as a socially accepted way of earning a living, whereas for the brighter working-class girl, who had always had to work, it gave the opportunity to rise above her usual work expectations.

The problems beset by this influx of office workers, both male and female, have been widely stressed, particularly emphasising the impact made on this once male domain by the ever increasing numbers of women. Nevertheless, the structural shift that had taken place in the Victorian economy towards the service or tertiary sector, created a demand for a vast expansion which was to continue well into the twentieth century. The overall consensus of opinion had constantly been the importance and therefore the need for commercial education in this country, but it was persistently encompassed with the general movement in support of technical education. Acceptance for the need for commercial education has been seen as a struggle against, not only the general attitude of society, but also the education world. The problems facing this country were two-fold. One by the fact that Britain, as the world's industrial leader, allowed a complacency to rule with the general feeling that education beyond the three R's was not necessary and held inherent dangers. The second stumbling block was attitude. It was widely held that the 'classic' type of education was the only possible grounding for the upper-class boys who would lead the country. Commercial education was barely given any consideration at all, and when it was, was merely considered as inferior and second-rate. Contrary to this view, the continental countries had long since been aware of the importance of technical and commercial education, borne out by the existence of the numbers of institutes of commerce that were to be found throughout the Continent as well as the United States.

By their very struggle, it may be argued that office workers have had more influence on educational work than most. The very nature of office work cannot be undertaken by any who have not the minimum general education comprised by the three R's and many employers, particularly the Civil Service as the largest, required an education above the minimum.[65] An overview of the situation shows that provision for commercial education was catered for by the initiatives of local forces. Whilst Sadler stressed that 'much that was attempted in evening schools would have been better done by a well-planned system of day schools'[66] nevertheless these endeavours, through the mechanics' institutes, chambers of commerce, private schools as well as the higher grade, together with the efforts of the Royal Society of Arts and other examining bodies that followed, helped create a workforce that was needed to advance into the twentieth century.

Notes

The place of publication is London unless otherwise stated.

1 M. E. Sadler, *The King's Weigh House Lectures to Businessmen* 1901, p. 28.

2 PP *Schools Inquiry Commission 1867–68*, VIII, p. 189.

3 Philip Magnus, *Industrial Education*, 1888, p. 80.

4 M. A. Dalvi, 'Commercial Education in England during 1851–1902', University of London, unpublished PhD thesis, 1956.

5 *Ibid*. p. 401.

6 Correlli Barnett, *The Collapse of British Power*, 1972, p. 95.

7 *Journal*, Royal Society of Arts, February 1979, p. 121.

8 *Ibid*. p. 122.

9 Eric Hopkins, *A Social History of the English Working Classes 1815–1945*, 1979, p. 71.

10 W. G. Blackie, *Commercial Education*, Glasgow, 1888, p. 7.

11 R. J. Montgomery, *Education and Commerce*, 1910, p. 6.

12 W. G. Hall, 'The Provision of Technical Education in Sunderland before 1908', University of Durham, unpublished MEd thesis, 1965.

13 J. Stuart Maclure, *Educational Documents. England and Wales 1816–1963*, 1965, p. 89.

14 *Ibid.* p. 112–13.

15 Dalvi, 'Commercial Education', p. 378.

16 See J. Stuart Maclure, *Educational Documents*, p. 148: 'As late as 1895 the Bryce Commissioners were pointing out the 'disadvantages from which you Englishmen suffer in industry and commerce'.'

17 *Hansard, 1887.*

18 Dalvi, 'Commercial Education', p. 304.

19 J. Leinster-Mackay, 'The advance of banausic education: some reflections on private commercial schools of Victorian England', *The Vocational Aspect of Education*, XXXIII, No. 84, 1979, p. 21.

20 W. Spens (Chairman), *Report of the Consultative Committee on Secondary Education with Special Reference to Grammar Schools and Technical High Schools*, 1939, p. 26.

21 PP *First Report of the Civil Service Inquiry Commission 1875*, XXIII, p. 6.

22 O. G. Pickard, 'Office work and education 1848–1948', *Vocational Aspect of Secondary & Further Education*, Issue 17, Nov. 1949, p. 231.

23 *Prospectus*, Skerry's College 1878–1958, pp. 16–18.

24 *Ibid.*, p. 22.

25 J. W. Godwin, 'The Bradford Mechanics' Institute', in Barnett Blake, *The Mechanics' Institutes of Yorkshire, 1859*, p. 344.

26 Edward Royale, 'The M.I. and the working classes, 1840–1860', *The Historical Journal*, XIV, 2, 1971, p. 305.

27 *Gateshead Guardian*, 11 June 1896.

28 George B. Hodgson, *The History of South Shields*, 1903.

29 *South Shields Gazette*, 31 July 1963.

30 Alexander Morgan, *Rise and Progress of Scottish Education*, 1927, p. 210.

31 *Ibid.*, p. 211.

32 PP *Final Report of the Commissions appointed to Enquire into the Elementary Education Acts, England & Wales, 1886*, p. 308.

33 Alexander Curr, 'The Scottish Education Department and commercial education in secondary schools', *The Secondary School Journal*, Edinburgh, January 1908.

34 *The Clerk*, 1908 (The National Union of Clerks' official publication).

35 *Journal*, RSA, 1853–56, IV, p. 587.

36 See Robert J. Montgomery, *Examinations*, 1965, pp. 76–184; John P. C. Roach, *Public Examinations in England 1850–1900*, 1971, p. 68, and David Lockwood, *The Blackcoated Worker*, 1958.

37 Ann M. Garnham, 'Education for Industry – The Newcastle Experience 1889–1902', unpublished M.Phil thesis, Sussex University, 1976.

38 PP *Report on the Census 1871.*

39 David Lockwood, *The Blackcoated Worker*, 1958, p. 124.

40 Alan Delgado, *The Enormous File. The Social History of the Office*, 1979, p. 72.

41 PP *1871 XXXVII (c.304 Report on the Reorganisation of the Telegraph System.*

42 *Ibid.*

43 Lee Holcombe, *Victorian Ladies at Work. Middle-class working women in England & Wales 1850–1914*, Newton Abbot, 1973, p. 162.

44 Anna Davin, 'Genteel Occupations in late 19th century London. Class and employment of women' (unpublished draft – undated), p. 32.

45 V. Karsland, *Women and their Work*, 1891, p. 138.

46 Letter, Prudential Assurance Co. Ltd., London, 13 February 1985.

47 Wigham Richardson, *Memoirs*, 1911, p. 283.

48 Alan Delgado, *The Enormous File*, p. 73.

49 Grace McNicol, *Teaching Shorthand & Typewriting*, 1964, p. 3.

50 Letter, Library Research Dept., House of Commons, London, 22 May 1984.

51 T. Kelly, *George Birkbeck, Pioneer of Adult Education*, 1947, p. 15.

52 Gregory Anderson, *Victorian Clerks*, 1976, p. 101.

53 G. L. Anderson, 'The Social Economy of Late-Victorian Clerks' in G. Crossick (ed.) *The Lower Middle-Class in Britain*, 1977, p. 127.

54 Margaret Mulvihill, 'The White-Bloused Revolution', MA Research Essay, London University, 1981, p. 8.

55 Anna Davin, 'Genteel occupations', p. 35.

56 *Phonetic Journal*, 4 April 1891, p. 209.

57 Alan Delgado, *The Enormous File*, pp. 37, 38.

58 *Newcastle Weekly Chronicle*, 6 January 1900.

59 O. G. Pickard, 'Office Work & Education 1848–1948', p. 232.

60 Leslie Hannah, *The Rise of the Corporate Economy*, 1976, p. 23.

61 W. J. Reader, *Professional Men. The Rise of the Professional Classes in 19th Century England*, 1966, p. 140.

62 Carlo M. Cipolla (ed.), *The Fontana Economic History of Europe*, Vol. 4, 1973, p. 802.

63 R. J. Montgomery, *Examinations*, p. 21.

64 O. G. Pickard, 'Office Work & Education 1848–1948', p. 238.

65 *Ibid*, p. 241.

66 M. E. Sadler, *Continuation Schools in England and Elsewhere. Their place in the educational system of an industrial and commercial state*, Manchester, 1907, p. 2.

5 Meta Zimmeck

'Get out and get under':[1]
the impact of demobilisation on the Civil Service, 1918-32

Demobilisation at the end of the First World War is a historian's black box. Inputs and outputs are readily ascertainable – servicemen and 'civil war workers' go into one end, and men and women in their 'normal' spheres of activity come out of the other – but what happens inside the box, the process of transformation, is something of a mystery. The traditional view is that in a series of voluntary and complementary movements, men and women resumed their prewar places.[2] As recent work has suggested[3], this view is insufficiently critical and informed by more than a little wishful thinking. Demobilisation was not so much a relaxation into 'normalcy' as an attempt to recreate it by main force. In the construction of reconstruction, government played a leading role,[4] never more so, as this paper will demonstrate, than in the Civil Service, where it exercised the dual functions of employer and regulator of the labour market. Demobilisation pitted three groups against each other – or rather it injected a new group, ex-servicemen,[5] into the on-going struggle between elite men and aspirant women for the implementation of a programme of equal opportunities and hence control of the Civil Service. On the whole the men stuck together. Ex-servicemen appeared on the scene at an opportune moment, when women were in a strong tactical position due to wartime 'substitution' and were threatening to translate this into solid gains. Although elite men at times found coping with their gallant allies a strain, they recognised that they were nevertheless a godsend, willing and eager cannon fodder in the war between the sexes which resumed, as it were, after the Armistice: 'The Coalition Government has only managed to stir up a violent sex antagonism, and concentrated the energies of the ex-serviceman on a valiant attempt to fight his sisters'.[6] Thus in the black box there were wheels within wheels, a text and a subtext.

From the beginning the organisation and staffing of the Civil Service have been controversial, the stuff of heated debate and innumerable investigations. With regard to the incorporation of women, the battle lines were drawn well before the First World War and have remained remarkably consistent ever since.[7] The male elite of the Civil Service, spearheaded by the Treasury, which formally supervised establishment matters, believed that the correct position for women was subordinate to men – i.e. selfless, patient, nitpicking drones and not commanding queen bees. Not unnaturally as employers the male elite wanted a staff which was efficient, cheap and tractable and after some consideration decided that the employment of women would promote this goal. Due to the restricted and intensely competitive nature of women's work in the late nineteenth century, the Treasury (like other employers) found that women were better qualified, cheaper, less experienced (and supposedly less interested) in trade union agitation than their male counterparts, and, moreover, could be used as a stick to beat recalcitrant men. The male elite began employing women as telegraphists in 1870 and gradually employed them on other 'manipulative', clerical, and, exceptionally, quasi-administrative work throughout the Civil Service (though the great bulk were employed in the Post Office) – but only in women's posts, classes, branches, departments and with special terms of service such as unequal pay, the marriage bar and restrictions on mobility. By the Edwardian period they were satisfied with the performance of women civil servants, satisfied by the economies effected through their employment, and satisfied with the divisive impact of their presence on staff unionism, and as a result they concluded that it was time to progress beyond the experimental stage.

Although the future position of women was the subject of considerable debate within the upper reaches of the Civil Service, the consensus was that change, whatever the details of departmental allocation, conditions of service, and pay, should be quantitative rather than qualitative, an increase in women's numbers but not in their penetration of the hierarchy. The Royal Commission on the Civil Service, which sat under the chairmanship of Lord Macdonnell from 1912 to 1914, considered the matter extensively, including submissions from women civil servants and their supporters. The Majority Report (2 April 1914) attempted to cut the ground from under the women's arguments for equal opportunities by denying that women's capacities were equal to men's 'in power of sustained work, in the continuity of service, and in adaptability to varying service conditions'. It then gave elite men a free hand to uphold the structural status quo: '. . . the object should be, not to provide employment for women as such, but to secure for the State the advantage of the services of women whenever those services will best promote its interests'. Finally, it disposed of women's access to higher posts by recommending an inquiry as to 'the situations . . . which might with advantage to the Public Service be filled by women', although, most importantly, not by open competition. The Minority Report favoured the expansion of women's employment both at the top and bottom of the grading structure but not in the middle.[8]

Towards the end of the First World War, the Treasury's Committee on Recruitment for the Civil Service after the War, appointed in late

whole women demonstrated flexibility, competence, tenacity, and even 'the attitude of command'. Indeed, wartime service, in giving them opportunities beyond their wildest dreams, whetted their appetites for real careers[15] and reinforced their determination to wrest something for themselves from the postwar settlement.

If, in the years before 1914, top civil servants viewed the employment of women with cautious approval, they were less than enthusiastic about the employment of ex-servicemen. The Treasury was urged by its brother departments, the War Office and, to a lesser extent, the Admiralty, to provide posts in the Civil Service for retired members of HM Forces. The service departments claimed that this prospect of continued employment was necessary to attract men of requisite calibre to the Forces and to keep them available afterwards for the Reserves. They claimed that the dead-end nature of military service and ex-servicemen's subsequent difficulties in reintegrating into civil society, – 'the degree to which Army or Navy service has reduced their capacities for earning their living on the open market'[16] – would be overcome by integrating military and civil service of the state: '[The ex-serviceman] has given a good deal of his life to the State and he is not joining another firm, he is joining the same firm again'.[17] As a sweetener the service departments alleged that the employment of ex-servicemen would benefit Civil Service management as well, since it would provide 'a practically inexhaustible supply of well-disciplined and responsible young men, who would not be likely to quarrel with their Bread and Butter'.[18] The Treasury's response to these blandishments was lukewarm. It was chary of using Civil Service employment as a reward for colour service and of recruitment in bulk by extraordinary means, but it acquiesced on the grounds that the employment of ex-servicemen would be restricted to non-clerical,[19] chiefly postman,[20], posts. Moreover, the Civil Service employers' experience of ex-service employees did nothing to change – and indeed confirmed – this view of their limited utility. Ex-servicemen, even though carefully vetted as to their 'parchment', proved an unprepossessing lot. They were more disruptive than civilian staff and more likely to be prosecuted or dismissed for disciplinary offences.[21] They were more likely to suffer from venereal diseases, which entailed extra costs (financial and moral) to their employers.[22] Finally they were not particularly good at their jobs – 'below average' seems to have been the consensus. On the whole ex-servicemen did not live up to the service departments' encomia, and by

1914 the Treasury was prepared to accept them only as a necessary, but minor, evil.

After the Armistice ex-servicemen[23] campaigned for employment in the battlefield style to which they were accustomed. Ex-servicemen belligerently ignored the elite's plans and the rather equivocal record of their predecessors and made simple but enormous demands. They wanted all posts – temporary posts, including those already filled as well as any created in future, and most permanent posts upon vacancy, including many already classed as 'suitable for women' – and they wanted these posts with a minimum of bureaucratic interference, no age bars and allocation rather than selection.[24] Their goal was full employment for themselves, if necessary at the expense of those persons whose contribution to the war effort was not on the same plane as their own, and they argued that normal recruitment should be suspended until this goal was achieved.

Ex-servicemen's method of campaign was unorthodox and of dubious propriety. Ex-servicemen organised themselves into powerful and vociferous lobbying organisations – the National Association of Discharged Sailors and Soldiers, the Comrades of the Great War, the British Legion, the Association of Ex-Service Civil Servants (AECS) – and these bodies kept up a barrage of complaints, exhortations, and threats aimed at all levels of the government – ministerial, Parliamentary, bureaucratic. At the highest level there were suave pleas from the likes of Field Marshal Earl Haig.[25] At the lowest level there were pathetic *cris de coeur* from desperate men. Most fruitfully, ex-servicemen focused their campaign on MPs, especially those 'service' MPs who entered Parliament via the Khaki Election of 1918[26], and sought to enlist them as a battering ram to open the doors, front and back, of the Civil Service.[27] Although bringing pressure to bear on government was, of course, a fundamental political strategy, it was in this instance pushed to lengths not contemplated before the war and couched along lines indistinguishable from patronage, repaying a debt, albeit the nation's debt.

Ex-servicemen advanced their claims not so much by a reasoned statement of their case as by attacking their 'enemies', 'rabbits' and 'pin money limpets'. They refused to recognise the legitimacy of non-servicemen's exemptions from military service (be they reservation for work of national importance, medical unfitness, and unavoidable detainment in POW camps) and castigated these 'embusques' for cowardice and self-aggrandisement:

They dug themselves well in for every big job that came their way . . . The clerical nonentities of 1914 were now big men and there was a sort of unwritten understanding among them to hold together to defend their new positions . . . practically every fat job in the Civil Service to-day is held by a young man who shirked the war.[28]

Ex-servicemen also attacked women for their 'selfishness' and 'unwomanliness' in preferring 'to wield a pencil when [they] might have wheeled a pram'.[29] They persistently characterised woman as pin-money workers not dependent on their earnings for their livelihoods and asserted that they could give up their jobs without any hardship:

Therefore, I ask you, young lady, who are now able to wear expensive hats and gloves and shoes and stockings to just stop and think a minute – think of the hundreds of acres in France adorned with small wooden crosses; think of the agonies some of the bodies under those crosses endured . . .; think of the cripples you see around you wherever you go; think of the ragged starving men who exist in thousands in every large city, and then, having considered all this, don't you think that cotton stockings will do instead of silk ones, and your last year's hat will suffice for this year? I am sure that the thought of your denying yourself these luxuries in giving up your job for one of these men who has done so much for you, will be more than enough reward.[30]

They also threatened that if women did not go voluntarily then, in the words of Sir William Robertson, they should be 'readjusted'.[31] Thus ex-servicemen's primary consideration was not promoting the 'good of the Service' but in securing 'the amenities of life'[32] for themselves. Ex-servicemen baldly demanded from the Civil Service what no other group of persons had demanded before, a reward for some service external to the Civil Service and without reference to its needs or requirements, and they attempted to get what they wanted in a way no other group had before, through irregular channels and at the expense of other groups which had no less right to consideration.

The Treasury's well publicised reconstruction plan and the demands for priority of ex-servicemen caused women civil servants great anxiety and frustration. Women civil servants understood that their position at the end of the war was for the moment favourable – they were already in post and their numbers, swollen by the wartime influx of temporary staff, made them a force to be reckoned with – but was likely to become less favourable over time due to reductions in staffing and reorganisation. They felt, therefore, that consolidation of their position was a matter of some urgency. Every moment of delay meant a consequent loss of advantage:

The chances given to us of proving our ability during the war, and the splendid hopes which the election pledges of the Government had raised in our hearts, were all vanishing into thin air, and one by one, slowly and insidiously, each office was reorganising its work, and everywhere women were being dispensed with or relegated to routine work, and so once more brought into economic dependency on their male relatives.[33]

To women civil servants the reconstruction scheme put a new gloss on old inequality. Though it held some attractions in that it 'practically laid down that women were to be relegated to routine work'[34], it was unacceptable in that it denied women access to the highest, most powerful, and most desirable posts:

There is a tendency on the official side still to continue the differentiation between men and women, and still to say that only a certain number of posts shall be limited to women – that a certain small proportion of the posts for Division 1 and Division 2 only are to go to women, and that the major proportion of the posts are to go to men. Ability is not to be the test for posts in Division 1, but sex.[35]

Women civil servants had been second-class employees long enough, they felt, and now, having achieved first-class citizenship by virtue of the vote, they were not prepared to remain in a new, if improved, clerical ghetto.

To women civil servants, however, ex-servicemen presented a new and more insidious threat. For social and psychological reasons women were conditioned to believe in their own inferiority, the lesser importance of their work and needs and the 'naturalness' of taking second place to men, and this psychological handicap was increased by the apotheosis of the 'hero' and 'warrior'. Though women civil servants after nearly half a century of confidence-raising felt reason-ably comfortable in asserting themselves against their male colleagues, and indeed gave every indication of enjoying a good scrap, they were desperately uncomfortable in doing so against ex-servicemen, many of whom were marked in mind and body by their terrible experiences. They were particularly sensitive to taunts in the press and in person about their 'lack of honour and decency' in clinging to work when those with a 'higher' claim needed their jobs. Women civil servants, then, were unable to resist ex-servicemen's aggression with feminist aggression, and they could not fight for jobs on the same level of selfish bravado as ex-servicemen. Such tactics were unacceptable to women themselves and would certainly have brought them profound public disapproval.

Instead women civil servants developed a defensive strategy, which, while not ceasing to press for equality of opportunity, sought to extract

the maximum possible advantage from distinctly unfavourable circumstances. In effect, they presented their claim for consideration in
terms which, harking back to wartime propaganda, were akin to those
used by ex-servicemen – their sacrifices, their needs, and debts of
honour owed to them. In the first place, they asserted that their losses
were, if not as great as those who made the ultimate sacrifice of their
lives, nevertheless large and worthy of recognition. Women's lives too
had been altered by the war – loved ones had been killed or wounded
or lost; the rigours of life and work on the home front had taken their
toll of physical and mental resources; the world for women too would
never be the same. The state, they said, 'should provide something for
those who have been damaged financially by the war in just the same
way as the State owes its obligations to the men who have lost their
livelihoods owing to the war'. Moreover, they carefully divided ex-
servicemen into categories of service and refused to pay exaggerated
homage to non-combatants, 'men who did not even leave England'.[36]
Indeed they scored satirical points at the expense of these 'Cuthberts':

> Right through the war in khaki so brave . . .
> In Whitehall did I work and slave . . .
> Though no great danger I may have seen . . .
> I might have been bombed in Parsons Green . . .
> A record like that should guarantee . . .
> Government pay for life for me.[37]

In the second place, women civil servants stated their claim in terms
not so much of their right to work as of their 'need' to work, which was
exacerbated by the war. They argued that scarce work necessarily
should be allocated in order of greatest need, irrespective of sex – i.e. (in
order of priority) to those persons who were disabled, then those who
supported dependents, those who supported themselves, and finally
those with independent means.[38] In so doing they attempted to break
the stranglehold of the 'family' versus 'single' model of men's and
women's employment and to reduce considerably the pool of 'heroes'
and 'breadwinners' to whom they would have to defer. Finally,
gritting their teeth, women civil servants defended the boundaries of
women's work as defined by the Treasury. In this way, they harked
back to the numerous pledges made in Parliament and in departments,
and the definition of work in grades, branches or departments as
'appropriate to women'. Facilitating the segregation of work was
hardly their ideal, but with ex-servicemen looking over the fence,
women were forced to hide behind the Gladstone Committee's scheme

and make pious applications to the Treasury for the defence of their preserve.

Despite the din, the Treasury resolved to get on with the implementation of its own scheme for the post-war Civil Service under the camouflage of demobilisation. To begin with, in the large-scale exercise of substitution, the Treasury used unestablished or temporary posts to provide jobs for ex-servicemen and thereby block women's progress towards equal opportunities. Temporary staff had been employed in small numbers before the First World War, sometimes

Table 5.2   *Size and composition of temporary/unestablished staff*

Date	Total staff	Women		Men		Ex-servicemen		
		Numbers	*% of total*	*Numbers*	*% of total*	*Numbers*	*% of total*	*% of men*
Mar. 1914	114,792	—	—	—	—	—	—	—
Nov. 1918	243,965	—	—	—	—	—	—	—
Mar. 1919	193,972	137,720	71	56,252	29	—	—	—
July 1919	179,332	115,061	64	64,268	36	—	—	—
July 1920	121,833	62,237	51	59,466	49	42,919	35	72
July 1921	114,078	46,076	40	68,002	60	59,002	52	87
July 1922	74,543	25,024	34	49,519	66	45,189	61	91
July 1923	61,617	19,517	32	42,100	68	39,218	64	93
July 1928	108,675	29,430	27	79,245	73	30,282	28	38
Apr. 1938	114,257	31,996	28	82,261	72	44,307	39	54

Sources: Data from the following sources (computations by the author): T162/111/E4345/2, 'Memorandum relating to the employment of ex-servicemen in the civil service', November 1920; Drake, table III; PP 1914 (418), lii, 557–60; 1914 (390), lvi, 537–9; 1919 Cmd. 276, xxxiv, 1249–54; 1919 Cmd. 316, xxxiv, 1255–7; 1920 Cmd. 598, xxx, 943–4; 1920 Cmd. 868, xxx, 953–4; 1920 Cmd. 879, xxx, 989–91; 1921 Cmd. 1495, xxxiii, 605–6; 1922 Cmd. 1762, iii, 125–7; 1923 Cmd. 1942, xvii, 829–31; 1928–9 Cmd. 3189, xiv, 771–3; 1937–8 Cmd. 5816, xx. 805.

while decisions were being made as to whether a new grade (e.g. typists, national insurance officers) would be made permanent, but more often for non-clerical messenger or 'outdoor' work in departments such as the Post Office, War Office, or Customs and Excise, and, as noted above, some of the officers in this latter category were pensioned-off soldiers and sailors. What was new about substitution after the First World War was the large number of temporary *clerical* posts available and the assignment to them of ex-servicemen. What was complicated about substitution was that it took place while wartime departments were being run down and staff, in consequence, reduced, so that it involved replacing women staff with men staff, while at the same time reducing the size of the temporary staff overall.

The guidelines governing substitution and the mechanism for implementing it were established by the Interdepartmental Committee on the Employment of Disabled Men in Government Departments, appointed on 6 June 1919 and chaired by the Treasury's Malcolm Ramsay. Working on the premise that it was 'a matter of national importance' to provide employment for ex-servicemen for a few years until industry 'may be expected to revive', the Ramsay Committee in its report (30 July 1919) defined certain posts as 'substitutable' (i.e. excluding those 'peculiarly appropriate to, or normally performed by, women' and those occupied by dependents of deceased or disabled servicemen) and recommended the appointment of ex-servicemen to these posts and the appointment of disabled ex-servicemen to a minimum of 8 per cent of the total. It established hierarchies for dismissal of existing staff based on need (first persons with independent means; then persons hired after the Armistice; and finally married women, except widows, hardship cases or those 'pivotal' or 'indispensable' persons with special skills) and for hiring based on military experience (first disabled, then combatant ['overseas'], and finally non-combatant ['home'] ex-service personnel).[39] These guidelines were confirmed by the First Interim Report (19 August 1920) of the Committee on the Appointment of Ex-Servicemen to Posts in the Civil Service, appointed on 21 July 1920 and chaired by Lord Lytton,[40] which considered matters affecting both temporary and permanent staff. However, after having been recalled twice due to complaints by the ex-servicemen's lobby, the Lytton Committee in its Third Report (14 June 1921) fudged somewhat on the definition of substitutable posts. It failed, as it were, firmly to defend the boundaries of 'women's posts' in the writing assistant grade or in the Ministry of Pensions' Pensions Issue Office and it made small but significant alterations in the rules for dismissal and hiring with the effect that women had to prove why they should not be dismissed and ex-servicemen, why they should not be hired.[41] These guidelines, as amended, continued in force until 1932.

The practice of substitution was not as orderly and judicious as the Ramsay and Lytton Committees' schemes would suggest, since the urgency of the problem, the muddle of makeshift arrangements and the constant interference of ex-servicemen's organisations took their toll. The 'donkey work'[42] of substitution was done by the Central Selection Board (CSB) of the Ministry of Labour (1919 and 1920) and then by the Joint Substitution Board of Labour (JSB) and the Treasury (1920 to 1932), together with their subsidiary departmental boards.[43] This involved the investigation of the suitability of posts for substitution and then the interviewing and placement (and often re-placement) of candidates in those posts. It was high pressure work. Officers of the boards sought to please their political and departmental superiors and had to deal with their own emotional responses, which veered between irritation with and pity for their difficult clients.

The vast majority of ex-soldier applicants [the CSB] had to deal with were workless and disabled, often on the verge of starvation for many had been discharged some time, and were suffering from real or imaginary grievances which the disappointment of a 'rejection' had the unfortunate result of instantly fanning into flame. These early days, therefore, were the days of 'scenes'.[44]

At the liaison meetings held with representatives of ex-servicemen's and women's organisations there was 'Bedlam'.[45]

These meetings were designed to allow both sides to put their views and so to ensure fair play, but this was an ever-receding goal. Ex-servicemen seized the initiative and turned these meetings into a sort of inquisition in which women staff were called upon to justify, as it were, their very existence, and the boards to account for their 'progress'. Ex-servicemen delved minutely into the personnel and workings of the various departments. They congratulated some departments for vigorous substitution (like, unsurprisingly, the Civil Service Commission, where substitution took place with 'lightning rapidity'[46]) and castigated others for slackness (to the extent of compiling a black list), denouncing the odd 'hot bed of female intrigue,[47] sniffing into persons' private lives (income, marital status, family responsibilities, grounds for exemption from military service), naming names, pointing fingers.[48] In addition, they attempted to bend the rules of substitution in order to give themselves additional advantages. They suggested that, while the Government was obliged to honour its pledges to ex-servicemen, 'it was justified in getting out of [them] if necessary where the women are concerned'.[49] They blurred the lines between the various kinds of military service and between the various kinds of women's need and argued that all ex-servicemen had priority over all women. They demanded that military pensions should not be counted as 'independent means'.[50] In short, substitution was difficult to implement in a calm and careful manner and was, in fact, the occasion for some very unpleasant harassment of women and non-service staff by ex-servicemen.

Despite this pressure by ex-servicemen and the Treasury's commitment in principle to discharging 'the national obligations to the ex-service man',[51] it nevertheless brooked no interference with its plans for the reorganisation of the Civil Service. While allowing ex-servicemen a free run in departments which were about to be liquidated or where work was transitory, it excluded them most particularly from 'women's work' in reserved grades and branches. The Treasury planned that the writing assistant grade, which had been introduced into some departments before the war after a protracted battle with women's associations and was planned for other departments upon reorganisation, would be the foundation of its pyramid. It declared that this grade would take over (from male assistant clerks and other analogous departmental grades) the mechanical and monotonous work 'which experience has shown . . . for both physical and psychological reasons is badly performed by men who not only work less quickly and accurately but form a thoroughly discontented staff'.[52] Despite the constant pressure of parliamentary questions and AECS memoranda, deputations, and claims in CSB and JSB liaison meetings, the Treasury held fast to its intention that writing assistant posts would be non-substitutable. Even when it was no longer possible to keep the grade out of the ring, the Lytton Committee in its Third Report in 1921 merely rehearsed the argument on both sides and made no findings,[53] so that the writing assistant grade remained inviolate, though subject in practice to nibbling at the departmental level.

The Treasury viewed the Ministry of Pensions and the Ministry of Labour as prototypes of modern 'mechanical' departments (as opposed to 'intellectual' departments such as itself) where much work was done on a large scale in large units and was hence 'suitable to women' and also suitable for downgrading to the writing assistant (or departmental equivalent) level. Work had been done in these departments by women since the beginning, so there was no rooted tradition of male occupancy. Ministerial pledges had been made that after the war these would be 'mainly' women's branches, and the Treasury intended, despite the assiduous campaign by ex-servicemen, that these pledges would be honoured, at least to the extent that it was convenient,

Any proposal further to impair the pledges given . . . would disturb the existing staff to an extent which would not be without its serious effect on the quality of work . . . [There should be] further substitution only if the position outside the Ministry is so serious as to require the laying down of a general rule that all temporary women clerical employees are to be discharged to make room for ex-servicemen.[54]

Under the terms of the Third Lytton Report, Pensions and later Labour were obliged to dismiss women until they constituted a mere 33 per cent (later reduced to 22 per cent) of the total staff. But the departments simply transferred women from other branches and concentrated them in the Pensions Issue Office and the Claims and Record Office, respectively, at Kew. This policy of dismissals and concentration, 'demobilising the bulk of the trained women . . . except for the higher grade women, who were to be relegated to routine work',[55] was vigorously resisted by women, both temporary and permanent, who saw it quite rightly as a method of depriving them of their hard-won gains. Although this manoeuvre gained ex-servicemen between four and five thousand jobs, they remained unsatisfied that such large prizes had escaped their grasp and so enormous was their appetite that, incensed by this 'duplicity', they blockaded the Claims and Record Office for several weeks in February 1923 and threatened to send the Prime Minister all their war decorations.[56]

The male temporary staff taken on under these conditions was not surprisingly of a very poor standard, both absolutely in comparison with pre-war recruits and relatively in comparison with the women they replaced. Throughout the exercise of substitution, the Treasury and other departments maintained for public consumption that substitution, after allowing for 'a certain "rustiness" . . . due to . . . absence from civilian life', involved very little lowering in the quality of recruits and no injury to the Civil Service: '. . . we have assumed that in every case the Department will satisfy itself as to the efficiency of the Ex-Service man, for no ex-Service man should be substituted for a woman or a Non-Service man unless he is considered to be thoroughly efficient and competent to do the work'.[57] In the privacy of inter- and intra-departmental correspondence the Treasury knew by November 1920 – after the first full year of substitution – that all the desirable candidates had been snapped up and that there was 'nothing much left to be substituted' in the way of posts. Of the candidates processed by the CSB and JSB only 20 per cent even approached the pre-war standard of performance.[58] By the late 1920s, for example, the Post Office was feeling 'pessimistic' at the quality of its ex-service staff and was looking back with nostalgia to its pre-war intake of ex-professional servicemen and lamenting the poor quality of the 'ex-Hostilities men'.[59] Nevertheless, as the size of the temporary staff declined, the proportion of men and ex-servicemen increased, and that of women decreased. This domination of transitory and low grade posts by substandard ex-servicemen might, ultimately, have had little impact, had it only been of short duration. However, this was not the case, and the ex-servicemen, taken on in conditions of high emotion and low rigour, not only remained permanently in temporary posts but provided the pool from which established civil servants were recruited for nearly a decade.

The second part of the Treasury's scheme for the post-war reorganisation of the Civil Service was the recruitment of established staff, and, as with temporary staffing, the Treasury used ex-servicemen

Table 5.3 *Size and composition of permanent staff*

Date	Total staff	Women Numbers	% of total	Men Numbers	% of total	Ex-servicemen Numbers	% of total	% of men
Mar. 1914	167,628	—	—	—	—	—	—	—
Nov. 1918	176,545	—	—	—	—	—	—	—
July 1919	227,962	54,805	24	173,157	76	—	—	—
July 1920	246,988	56,663	23	190,325	77	81,345	33	43
July 1923	242,894	56,500	23	186,394	77	102,541	42	55
July 1928	193,138	44,782	23	148,356	77	101,405	53	68
Apr. 1938	262,234	69,410	26	192,824	74	128,534	49	67

Sources: As table 5.1.

as pawns in its game with women civil servants. In so doing the Treasury cynically manipulated its own entrance requirements in order to put ex-servicemen into blocking positions, and this deviation from normal practice increased rather than decreased over time. Thus, for example, the Treasury lowered the general standard of examination and the level of qualification, lengthened the duration of qualification, introduced innovations including current affairs questions, work assessment, and interviews, and delayed the reintroduction of competition. The process began with the directions given by the Sub-Committee on Temporary Staffs of the Reorganisation Committee of the National Whitley Council,[60] appointed on 14 October 1919, which recommended in its report (24 February 1920) that clerical vacancies in that year should be filled by means of a set of examinations in which candidacy would be limited to temporary staff under the age of thirty-five with one year's qualifying service either in HM Forces or in civil war work. The standard was to be that of the pre-war Civil Service, and 75 per cent of male vacancies were to be reserved for ex-servicemen.[61]

Before the male clerical examinations took place, the Treasury moved to conciliate ex-servicemen, who were outraged by what they felt was the paltriness of its proposals, by appointing the Lytton Committee, and in its successive reports the Lytton Committee decreased the height of the hurdles for ex-servicemen and increased the length of time that these special arrangements would obtain. Its First Interim Report (19 August 1920) recommended holding a one-off examination, as had the Reorganisation Sub-Committee, but it made a concession to the candidates' age and experience by adding a current affairs section (the 'jazz' questions) to the usual academic syllabus. It promised immediate appointment to those of 'competitive' standard and eventual appointment to those of 'qualifying' standard, a novelty in so far as in previous examinations the number of appointments was determined by the number of places available, and candidacy lapsed after a finite period. The Civil Service Commission (CSC) stated that 'any candidate of sufficient education and good natural intelligence should be able to make a good show',[62] but in practice, though the number of candidates was 'overwhelming', less than a quarter passed and many of these did so only because the Commission used its considerable discretionary powers to boost weak candidates, especially the disabled, over the qualifying line.[63] Despite this the AECS claimed that the examination had been rigged against them, that the Treasury had ten times as many posts available as it was offering to them, and that they should get another chance.[64] The Lytton Committee was once again set in motion and produced a Second Interim Report (29 March 1921) by which it scheduled a second examination for those unsuccessful in the first, set up an investigation board for unsuccessful candidates, allocated to them 70 per cent of vacancies, and authorised the resumption of open competitive examination in April 1922.

Far beyond the immediate aftermath of the war, the Treasury continued to make sweeping concessions. The Chancellor of the Exchequer's Committee on the Initial Salary of 'Lytton' Entrants and the Appointment of Ex-Service Men to Posts in the Civil Service, chaired by Lord Southborough, provided in its Final Report (5 June 1924) yet another 'go' for the unsuccessful. It further lowered the standard of examination and in addition allowed 25 per cent of the final mark to be made up by an evaluation of candidates' work. Again, it gave the assurance that all qualifying candidates would eventually receive posts and pushed back the date for the resumption of open competition to the end of 1924, six years after the end of the war.[65] Although the Southborough examination was to be the 'final solution',[66] the Treasury made a further concession to ex-servicemen. The Guinness Agreement[67] of 12 January 1925 provided that in addition to those candidates successful under the Southborough examination in July an equal number of the unsuccessful candidates would be transferred without any further exam to permanent non-pensionable posts in the 'P' Class with the right 'exceptionally' by promotion to enter the permanent grades.[68] Open competition for male clerical posts finally resumed in November 1927, nine years after the end of the war. Even then there remained a large body of ex-service temporaries who laboured on in insecurity. The Royal Commission on the Civil Service, chaired by Lord Tomlin, succumbed to the pathos and pleas of these 'poor things'[69] and the desire to tidy up loose ends, and in 1931 it recommended the winding-up of all temporary employment.[70] In consequence, members of the 'P' Class and the remaining temporary staff as of August 1932, were constituted the 'Special' or 'S' Class, a permanent obsolescent class.

Thus in the end, the Treasury satisfied the ex-servicemen's long-standing goal, assimilation for all ex-servicemen by co-option. In the first and second Lytton examinations in 1920 and 1922, 4,490 and 1,808 ex-servicemen, respectively, entered Treasury (common to the service) grades, and an additional 2,142 entered the departmental grades in a series of small-scale examinations. In the Southborough examination in 1925, 8,000 were successful and an additional 8,000 went into the 'P' Class, leaving a residue of about 7,000. These together made up the 'S' Class after 1932. Thus over 31,000 ex-servicemen entered the established clerical grades alone, and, allowing for attrition, by 1931 ex-servicemen constituted nearly 50 per cent of all civil servants and 60 per cent of all men in the clerical grades.[71]

The Treasury did not extend its curiously casual methods of recruitment of permanent staff to women, and indeed it treated temporary women who were seeking establishment with great severity. The Treasury faced two interrelated problems in terms of this process, those of quantity and quality. At the end of the war, there was a large pool of temporary women staff and within that another, smaller but still considerable, pool of able and experienced women who wished to make their careers in the Civil Service. These women were potentially both a resource and a threat, and the Treasury attempted to maximise the one and minimise the other in the following way. It decided to cream off the most able women and channel them into work 'suitable for women', the lower clerical grades and not the higher clerical, executive and administrative grades, which were, in fact, the levels at which many of them were already working in temporary posts and in which they without doubt aspired to be made permanent. In those lower grades the Treasury expected these ex-temporary women to form leadership cadres – capable, stable, committed. After the initial reconstruction intake, the Treasury wanted to return as soon as possible to the pre-war conditions of recruitment – that is, 'a sudden influx of young pig-tailed maidens'[72] – via straightforward open competitive examinations, in order to create a rank and file which was green wood as opposed to seasoned timber. The Treasury intended that the lower clerical grades would be efficient and well-led but not rebarbative, since the wartime massed phalanx of unionised, mature, experienced, and feisty women would have been gutted and, for the most part, disposed of.

The reconstruction recruitment of women, which was carried out against the background of satisfying ex-servicemen's claims, was carefully timetabled and structured to fulfil this intention. The Treasury quickly organised examinations for temporary women staff for the typing/shorthand-writing and writing assistant grades, which were all-women grades, and even then only after intentional delay and wilful obfuscation[73] for the clerical grade, and after further delay and even more obfuscation for higher grades (see below). This was for whipping-in purposes, to encourage women either to take themselves off into other fields or, if they wished to stay in the Civil Service, to lower their sights rather than wait for better opportunities.[74] In these examinations, the Treasury raised the qualifying standard in order to avoid an *embarras de richesse*. For example, in the Lytton clerical grade examination of October 1920, only 7 per cent of women passed and 20 per cent qualified.[75] Moreover, the Treasury did not promise eventual establishment to those reaching qualifying standard, as it did to ex-servicemen. In fact, one irate veteran of a Lytton examination likened it to a sweepstake: 'But, oh! the sublety of the promoters of this sweep – the number and value of the prizes has never yet been ascertained'.[76] Finally, the Treasury reinstated open competition. First it provided examinations for women only at an early date – 1922 for writing assistants and 1925 for clerical officers, and then later, for men and women. Only four joint competitive examinations for men and women for clerical posts were held between the end of the war and the Report of the Tomlin Commission in 1931 (1927, 1929, 1930 and 1931) and only three for executive posts (1928, 1930 and 1931), though afterwards they took place, for the most part, annually. Between 1919 and 1925, nearly 3,500 temporary women were established in the writing assistant grade in four limited competitions (with another 1,700 through open competition). Between 1919 and 1926, 3,000 were established in Treasury and departmental clerical grades in ten limited competitions (with another 1,100 through open competition). Thus only 6,500 women temporaries were appointed to permanent posts as compared with over 31,000 ex-servicemen. Put another way, this means that a woman employed in a temporary post on 1 July 1919 had a 6 per cent chance of being established by 1926, compared to a 48 per cent chance for an ex-seviceman similarly employed.[77]

If the Treasury was eager to shepherd women into the depths of the Civil Service grading structure, it was even more eager to divert them from the heights. Faced with the need to replenish the administrative grade, the Treasury was adamant in its determination to recruit on its own terms. Both women and ex-servicemen were shouldered out of the way in the rush to obtain 'the right sort of chaps' – i.e. men like those pre-war recruits already serving in the administrative grade. It held a series of 'reconstruction' examinations in 1919, 1920 and 1921, not under the terms of the Ramsay Committee or the Reorganisation Sub-Committee but under those of the Gladstone Committee, the only examinations so held. The successful candidates, bedecked with military *vice* academic honours completely fulfilled the Treasury's expectations. Over 1,327 men were appointed to higher posts by this route – 203 to the administrative grade (5 non-service); 68 to the Foreign Office and Diplomatic Service (2 non-service); 249 to the intermediate grade (no non-service); and 807 to the Customs and

Excise (2 non-service).[78] By this swift and vigorous action, the Treasury pre-empted the field, and consequently agitated ex-service-men – granted a special Class I examination, held in August 1921 under the terms of the Third Interim Report of the Lytton Committee – found themselves too late for the prizes: 'No group of candidates has received less reward for its efforts than the men who attended that Examination'. A total of 113 candidates stood, of whom 87 were ex-servicemen, but, most posts having been filled by 'reconstruction' entrants, only three men were appointed outright, two of whom were non-servicemen, and by September 1924 only eight had been appointed.[79] The AECS was quick to grasp the social implications of the exercise: it was an 'economic dodge to enable the "tin gods" of the Service to save their face when they succeed in their laudable object of keeping the Service uncontaminated by the proximity of the common herd'.[80]

The Treasury provided even fewer opportunities to gain high posts to temporary women and, in fact, procrastinated until October–December, 1922. It also played possum as to the nature of the examination – which grades it covered, whether it was a one-off or the first of a series, who was eligible. In the result the 'superclerical' examination included within its ambit all posts from the higher clerical upwards, but there was no indication given of the number and distribution of posts available – in fact, another sweepstake.[81] It was open not only to temporary women but also to permanent women (who unlike male established staff were obliged to take an additonal examination for promotion).[82] After a preliminary weeding by the Civil Service Commission, no less than 500 candidates sat the examination, but only four were appointed to administrative posts, three to the senior executive, two to the junior executive and sixteen to the higher clerical – a truly meagre haul. Moreover, the successful candidates, with the exception of Myra Curtis, who was the un-challenged victor in first place, were not taken off the list in strict order (as was the usual Civil Service practice) but were plucked off in a way which raised not a few eyebrows and suggested 'favouritism and jugglery-pokery'.[83] The recruitment of women to the administrative grade via selection procedures common to both men and women, which began in 1925, did not change the situation. The addition of the interview as a part of normal procedure gave the Treasury a new tool with which to defend the bastion of gentlemen, and only a trickle of women entered via open competition, thirty-five or 7 per cent of 490 appointments in the years 1925 to 1939, and by 1939 there were only forty-three women in the administrative grade, 3 per cent of the total.[84]

The 'demobilisation' recruitment of temporary and established staff ultimately determined the shape of the interwar Civil Service and the opportunities afforded to women. The priority of ex-servicemen in recruitment for nearly a decade effectively blocked moves by women civil servants to achieve greater scope and rewards for their services to the state. Women wanted and expected an increase in the number and range of posts for which they were eligible. Indeed, this was particularly the case in view of the trend of recommendations of the various bodies which investigated the issue – Macdonnell Commission, Gladstone Committee, the Women's Advisory Committee's Sub-Committee, the National Whitley Council's Reorganisation Committee – wartime pledges, and 'the spirit of the age'. The Treasury, however, thwarted these ambitions by making sure that these posts and potential posts were filled by others. The reconstruction examinations effectively blocked movement towards the top, and the Lytton and Southborough examinations and later co-options, as well as the maintenance of temporary staff and the 'reservation' of posts to one sex or the other, blocked consolidation downwards and movement sideways. As a result, women made no spectacular gains in the interwar period. They comprised 21 per cent of the Civil Service in 1914, 25 per cent in 1928, 27 per cent in 1938.[85] In 1932, 48 per cent were in grades or branches reserved to women.[86] Because the high age at entry of ex-servicemen skewed the age structure, there was an 'undue proportion of middle aged or elderly persons' among male staff, and, given men's prejudice against serving 'under' any women, this acted as a drag both on promotion and placement.[87]

In the end, the Treasury's policies on recruitment in the period of demobilisation were both a success and a failure. They were a success for the elite men of the Civil Service and, most particularly, for its shock troops – the men of the Treasury – who used them to protect their own privileged position against penetration by the socially undesirable, 'flappers' and the 'common herd'. These policies succeeded in containing the most urgent threat to the gentlemen of Whitehall, that of women – numerous, ambitious, and most of all already there in the Civil Service – by a combination of playing the ex-service card and delay. They succeeded even in dissipating, albeit in a more subtle fashion, the additional threat, that of 'other ranks' (working- and lower-middle-class men), by giving ex-servicemen their 'due' in such a way that though they gained posts they lost credibility. These policies were, however, a failure for the Civil Service as a whole, both as a bureaucratic machine and as a profession. They wantonly cheated of opportunity women, who might have proved 'a fresh and valuable source of strength'[88] and demoralised others, ex-servicemen. They cynically manipulated the examination system, which was the holy of holies of the Civil Service and in so doing revealed the self-aggrandisement of the 'tin gods' and the fragility of 'principles':

Why is it that the women, who desire a straight competitive examination, are selected by a committee not on their scholastic accomplishments, but on something else, whereas the ex-Service men, who have appealed for a selective test on their work and former military record, are refused it, and are told that it is opposed to the principles of the Civil Service.[89]

In this way these policies robbed the Civil Service of efficiency, dignity and morale. Thus in the black box of demobilisation, there were complicated manoeuvrings, shifting alliances, even spite marriages, and there ultimately emerged winners, the male mandarins, and losers, women, ex-servicemen, and the Civil Service.

Notes

1 'Song Interpretations: The Discharged Soldiers' Association to the Women Government Clerks', *Taxette: The Organ of the Association of Temporary Women Tax Clerks* [hereafter *Taxette*], 1, 1 (February 1920), p. 3.

2 This view was put forward at the time by, for example, Mary Macarthur: 'Although the women were never consulted when the pledges [for the restoration of pre-war trade union customs and conditions] were given, I cannot imagine that any organisation of women would think of asking they should not be redeemed. I am also certain that no individual woman will desire to retain the job of any soldier or sailor who may return to claim it'. 'Women's Work', *North Mail*, 11 September 1917, cited by Marian Kozak, 'Women Munition Workers during the First World War with Special Reference to Engineering' (unpublished PhD thesis, University of Hull, 1976), p. 327. And it has been reiterated more recently by Arthur Marwick: 'It has to be remembered that the understanding upon which most women took employment during the war was that of a temporary contribution to the National effort. There was an obligation to find jobs for soldiers returning from the trenches. Prejudices, of course, remained; but then, it was clearly the ambition of the vast majority of women to be wife and mother. The terrible tragedy of the war was that for so many of them this was denied'. *Women at War, 1914–1918* London, Fontana Paperbacks/Imperial War Museum, 1977, p. 163.

3   For this revisionist view see Kozak and Gail Braybon, *Women Workers in the First World War*, London and Totowa, N.J., Croom Helm, 1981. For the Second World War see Denise Riley, *War in the Nursery: Theories of the Child and Mother*, London, Virago, 1983; and Penny Summerfield, *Women Workers in the Second World War: Production and Patriarchy in Conflict*, London, Croom Helm, 1984. See also Gail Braybon and Penny Summerfield, *Out of the Cage: Women's Experiences in Two World Wars*, London, Pandora, 1987.

4   See Paul Barton Johnson, *Land Fit for Heroes: The Planning of British Reconstruction, 1916–1919*, Chicago, University of Chicago Press, 1968; and Philip Abrams, 'The Failure of Social Reform', *Past and Present*, 24 (1963), pp. 43–64.

5   The term 'ex-servicemen' in this context means those men released from service in HM Forces who were not previously civil servants; that is, it excludes civil servants returning to their posts after wartime service. For a discussion of demobilisation from ex-servicemen's point of view see Graham Wootton, *The Official History of the British Legion*, London, MacDonald and Evans, 1956; Stephen R. Ward, 'Great Britain: Land Fit for Heroes Lost' in Stephen R. Ward (ed.), *The War Generation: Veterans of the First World War*, Port Washington, N.Y. and London, Kennekat Press/National University Publications, 1975, pp. 10–37; and Andrew Rothstein, *The Soldiers' Strikes of 1919*, London, Journeyman Press, 1985 [1980].

6   'From the Office Window', *Woman Clerk: The Organ of the Association of Woman Clerks and Secretaries* (AWKS) [hereafter *Woman Clerk*], 1, 12 (November 1920), p. 129.

7   For the history of women civil servants see Dorothy Evans, *Women and the Civil Service: A History of the Employment of Women in the Civil Service, and a Guide to Present Day Opportunities*, London, Pitman & Sons, 1934; Hilda Martindale, *Women Servants of the State, 1870–1938: A History of Women in the Civil Service*, London, George Allen & Unwin, 1938; Elizabeth Brimelow, 'Women in the Civil Service', *Public Administration*, 59 (Autumn 1981), pp. 313–35; Samuel Cohn, *The Process of Occupational Sex-Typing: The Feminization of Clerical Labour in Great Britain*, Philadelphia, Temple University Press, 1985; Teresa Davy, '"A Cissy Job for Men; a Nice Job for Girls": Women Shorthand Typists in London, 1900–39' and Kay Sanderson, '"A Pension to Look Forward to . . .?": Women Civil Service Clerks in London, 1925–1939', in Leonore Davidoff and Belinda Westover (eds.), *Our Work, Our Lives, Our Words: Women's History and Women's Work*, Basingstoke, Macmillan Education, 1986, pp. 124–44 and 145–60, respectively. See also other articles by the author, 'Strategies and Stratagems for the Employment of Women in the British Civil Service, 1919–1939', *Historical Journal*, 27 (1984), pp. 901–24; 'We Are All Professionals Now: Professionalisation, Education and Gender in the Civil Service, 1873–1939', *Women, Education and the Professions, History of Education Society*, Occasional Publication, No. 8, 1987; and 'The New Woman in the Machinery of Government: A Spanner in the Works?' in Roy MacLeod (ed.), *Government and Expertise in Britain, 1815–1919: Specialists, Administrators and Professionals*, Cambridge University Press, 1988, pp. 185–202.

8   P.P. 1914 Cd.7338 xiv, Royal Commission on the Civil Service, Report, paras.19, 18, 27; Minority Report, paras. 38, 60.

9   PRO, T1/12315/17863/19, Committee on Recruitment for the Civil Service After the War [hereafter Gladstone Committee], Final Report, 22 April 1919, Pt. II.

10   T1/12265/50322 Pt.I/18, Gladstone Committee, minutes of 31st meeting, 13 November 1918, evidence of J. A. Flynn, Ministry of Pensions.

11   The Sex Discrimination (Removal) Act, 1919 provided that 'a person shall not be disqualified by sex or marriage from the exercise of a public function, or from being appointed to or holding any civil profession or vocation or from admission to any incorporated society'. After some fancy footwork, the Treasury obtained the Order in Council of 22 July 1920, which exempted the Civil Service from its provisions.

12   T1/12333/23481/19, Ministry of Reconstruction, Women's Advisory Committee, Sub-Committee to Consider the Position of Women in the Civil Service, Final Report, 3 January 1919.

13   Deputation [of the Association of Women Clerks and Secretaries] to the Prime Minister', 30 January 1920, *Woman Clerk*, 1, 3 (February 1920), p. 31, statement of Miss L. Withrington, lady superintendent, Pensions Issue Office. There is another account of this deputation in PRO, T162/16/E1035.

14   Martindale, p. 81.

15   Government departments for example, did not often make the mistake of asking women what they wanted to do after the war. In one survey conducted by the War Office 58 per cent of women clerks wanted to remain at work after the war, 30·5 per cent were not sure, and only 11·5 per cent did not want to continue. T1/12333/23481/19, Ministry of Reconstruction, Civil War Workers Committee, Final Report on Substitute Labour, para. 7.

16   POA, POST30/1413/E14849/1907 Pt. 5, Post Office to Admiralty, 1 March 1906.

17   PRO, T172/69, 'Deputation of Ex-Naval and Military Civil Service Association to the Chancellor of the Exchequer', 4 July 1912, statement of Lord Charles Beresford.

18   POST30/1802-03/E2913/1910 Pt. 8, memorandum, R. J. Rocke, 4 August 1890.

19   For example, 'military clerks', were employed by the War Office in its outstations, primarily for dealing with stores and the like, but even on these duties the War Office recognised that they were less efficient than civilians: 'I should doubt [their comparable efficiency] as a whole. They are slower. Of course they have knowledge which is useful in the examination of store accounts'. P.P. 1887 c. 5226 xix, Royal Commission on Civil Establishments, Minutes of Evidence, evidence of Sir Ralph Thompson, 9 December 1886, Q258.

20   The Post Office established various schemes for the employment of ex-servicemen. In 1872 it offered all vacancies for rural post messengers (i.e. postmen) to ex-soldiers, but there were very few takers and the scheme lapsed in 1878. In 1883 it offered posts created by the introduction of the parcel post service to ex-soldiers, but 'the Postmasters reported so adversely on the work of the ex-soldiers, that it was decided not to extend their employment'. In 1887 it offered vacancies in postman posts in certain Irish provinces to ex-soldiers, but the response was low and this scheme too lapsed. In the 'Raikes scheme' of 1891, it offered all vacancies in postman posts to ex-servicemen and required messengers wishing to become postmen to enlist and serve a tour of duty first. This met with 'strong protests' from parents of boy messengers and a massive decline in recruitment, and the scheme was abandoned after two years. In 1897 the Post Office adopted the 'alternate scheme' in which it reserved 50 per cent of vacancies in postman posts and London porter posts to ex-servicemen and the remaining 50 per cent to ex-messengers or other postal servants. The scheme included arrangements for offsetting appointments of ex-servicemen to sorting clerk and telegraphist and other manipulative posts against the quota. This scheme was still in operation at the end of the war, though the proportion of ex-servicemen had risen. POA, POST33/2174/M16683/1927 Pt. 2, 'Employment of ex-Service men in the Post Office', November 1926.

21 For example, in 1892 although ex-servicemen accounted for 24 per cent of all established postmen, they accounted for 24 per cent of prosecutions by the department for misconduct. POST30/1802-03/E2913/1910 Pt. 4, Post Office to War Office, 23 September 1893. Another, more detailed, survey in 1895 revealed that ex-servicemen were about twice as likely as their civilian colleagues to be dismissed overall; slightly less than three times, for drunkenness; six times, for fighting; four times, for insubordination; and two and a half times, for absence without leave. *Ibid.*, Pt. 20, 'Copy of Memorandum handed by P.M.G. to Secretary of State for War in connection with Mr Arnold Forster's Motion', April 1896. Calculations by the author.

22 'A considerable number of Army medical histories have passed through my hands now. I have been much struck by the high proportion of cases in which the Candidate has contracted syphilis or some kindred venereal disease'. POST30/2935/E9978/1914, S. J. Ching to E. Raven, 18 July 1912. The Post Office eventually required ex-service candidates for employment to take a Wassermann test.

23 Ex-servicemen did not enter the Civil Service in any great numbers until the summer of 1919, and they first formed departmental associations in the various departments in which their presence was greatest – the Ministries of Food, Munitions, and Labour. They then put together an umbrella organisation, the National Ex-Servicemen's Union of Temporary Civil Servants which became in turn the Joint Committee of Ex-Servicemen's Unions (Civil Service) and then the Association of Ex-Service Civil Servants.

24 There was no age limit, and 'only a superficial examination was required when you were wanted for the front line'. 'A Report of the Proceedings at a Mass Meeting of the National Ex-Service Men's Union of Temporary Civil Servants, held at Caxton Hall, Westminster, on Friday, the 18th June, 1920, at 6.0 p.m.', *Live Wire: The Official Organ of the National Ex-Service Men's Union of Temporary Civil Servants* [and successor organisations] [hereafter *Live Wire*], [I, 2] (July, 1920), statement of G. B. Lee. For a concise presentation of the AECS's programme see *Milestones in our Fight for Justice: What the Association of Ex-Service Civil Servants has Won for Ex-Service Men and What it Means to Win*, London, AECS, 1923.

25 Who urged that ex-servicemen be given the first claim on all unestablished posts, except cleaning, shorthand and typing posts which were to be left to women, and established lower clerical posts as a 'last resort'. Haig's view on women was instrumental: 'Allowance is made for the progress in the position of women during recent years, but it is felt that where women have acceded to positions entirely owing to the absence of men on War Service, these positions should be vacated by them in consequence of the men's return'. T162/79/E8053, Haig to Lloyd George, 12 March 1922).

26 And engaged in hieratic rituals of military bonding with Lieut-Col Sir Samuel Hoare, Cmdr Viscount Astor, and other honourable and gallant members. They even tried this act (with less success) on Cmdr Hilton Young, financial secretary to the Treasury.

27 MPs turned up regularly to meetings on ex-service issues. One in November 1921, on the subject of dismissals of ex-servicemen in the overall reduction of Civil Service staffs caused by the liquidation of wartime ministries, was particularly well attended: 'I do not think that I have ever seen a better attended committee meeting of Members drawn from all parties'. T162/73/E6967, Hoare to Young, Treasury, 21 November 1921. And they also fired volleys of Parliamentary Questions on ex-servicemen's behalf. In a typical week, 19–26 November 1920, four Parliamentary Questions were asked by service MPs on the hiring of temporary women staff rather than ex-servicemen in general and at the Ministry of Pensions in particular; and the use of overtime at the Post Office rather than hiring extra (i.e., ex-service) staff. T162/812/E828/1. The *Live Wire* regularly printed these Parliamentary Questions.

28 'A Permanent "Old Contemptible"', 'Permanents and the War: Young Shirkers who Dug Themselves in and Froze Out the Ex-Service Men', *Live Wire*, III, 34 (March 1923), pp. 49–50.

29 This is the punchline of an uninspired but revealing piece of doggerel: 'The world seems topsy-turvey since he left his pleasant (!) trench – / When he went, his little Gladys was a homely sort of wench, / But for home and homely comforts now she doesn't care a damn, / And prefers to wield a pencil when she might have wheeled a pram'. It concludes: 'Still a day may soon be coming in the blissful bye-and-bye, / As a grateful Country promised, and we know *that* cannot lie; / When the Heroes shall be welcome wherever they may go, / And Jane shall quit the office for the job of punching dough'. E. R. Gregory, 'Fit for Heroes Series, No. 5', *Live Wire*, [I], 4 (September 1920), p. 2.

30 H.W.G.W., 'An Appeal to Women who are Employed in Occupations which normally were held by Men', *Live Wire*, [I], 5 (October 1920), p. 11.

31 'My point is a simple one and has never varied. It is that woman has the same right to work and live as man. I detest the idea that women should be mere dolls and playthings. But all women are not now in their right places. Many got out of them in the War, and need readjusting; there is much work for women which women refused to do, and there are women in posts where, from any point of view, men should be.' Letter to Dorothy Evans, secretary, AWKS, *Woman Clerk*, 2, 4 (March 1921), p. 45.

32 As far as the ex-officer is concerned . . . the problem of unemployment is much more difficult of solution. His birth, education, and training entitled him to live up to a higher standard. He is, in fact, incapable of doing justice to any occupation that is calculated to deprive him of the amenities of life to which he has become accustomed'. T162/812/E828/4, Capt. E. N. St.J. Dickinson to J. Ramsay Macdonald, 13 July 1929.

33 'The Women's Procession', *Woman Clerk*, 1, 6 (May 1920), p. 64.

34 'Deputation to the Prime Minister', *Woman Clerk*, 1, 3 (February 1920), statement of Miss [L] Withrington, p. 31.

35 *Ibid.*, statement of Miss [Dorothy] Evans, p. 30.

36 *Ibid.*, pp. 29, 30.

37 'Awks Songbook: Man was not meant to work alone' [words by 'B. Jabbers' and sung to the tune of 'As I was going to Strawberry Fair'], *Woman Clerk*, 2, 8 (July 1921), pp. 89–90.

38 For the acme of pathos see the story, 'Ex-Service' by Bertha Hudson, in which Kitty, a temporary clerk supporting her mother (widowed in the war) and the child of her brother, killed on the Somme, receives her notice: 'In actual reality [her father and brother] are both Ex-Service men, yet if I lost my position who would care?' *Woman Clerk* 2, 2 (January 1921), pp. 19–20.

39 PRO, CSC5/114, Interdepartmental Committee on the Employment of Disabled Men in Government Departments, Report, 30 July 1919, para. 11 *et passim*. I am indebted to Dr N. G. Cox for this reference.

40 Two of its members had 'definite tickets' – Capt. C. E. Loseby, MP, to defend the interests of ex-servicemen and Mrs Ray Strachey, of women civil servants. T162/25/E1634/01, memorandum, M. G. Ramsay, 23 June 1920, approved by Stanley Baldwin, 24 June.

41 T162/25/E1634/04 Annexe, Committee on the Appointment of Ex-Service Men to Posts in the Civil Service [hereafter Lytton Committee], First [Interim] Report, paras. 13–18 *et passim*. and Third Interim Report, paras. 48–53, 18–19 *et passim*.

42 PRO, LAB2/2118/SB451 (pres.A/1331), E. C. Cunningham, Ministry of Labour, to M. G. Ramsay, Treasury, 27 August 1920.

43 The Treasury initially allowed the Ministry of Labour to organise substitution via the CSB on the grounds that Labour had considerable expertise in dealing with unemployment through its network of labour exchanges. Labour, however, in the Treasury's eyes, proved a bit too eager to be 'recognised as the agency for filling vacancies' and to effect substitution 'to the utmost possible extent' (i.e. including women's posts as defined by the Gladstone Committee, especially writing assistant posts. In 1920 the Treasury clawed back part control when, under the terms of the First Report of the Lytton Committee, it established the JSB, which had two members each from the Treasury and Labour and an 'independent' (non-Civil Service) chairman. Since each department declined to 'keep to its own pitch' and sought to increase its powers at the expense of the other, relations were often strained. LAB2/1900/CEB1330 (pres. C5/1925), A. S[teel] M[aitland], Labour, to W. Guinness, Treasury, 24 April 1924; T162/24/E1634/1, M. G. Ramsay to Stanley Baldwin, 7 September 1920; LAB2/2118/SB451 (pres. A/1331), T. J. Macnamara, Labour, to Hilton Young, Treasury, 14 November 1920, respectively. The AECS preferred a different 'independent' composition for the JSB and its satellites: one representative of the government, the AECS, and an outside ex-servicemen's organisation. George B. Lee, 'Substitution!!!', *Live Wire*, [I], 9 (February 1921), pp. 7–8.

44 CSC5/114, Claughton Kelly, 'A Record of the Work of the Civil Service Commission Representatives on the Central Selection Boards: The First 20,000', 18 October 1920.

45 Minutes of the JSB, 1920–22, are in LAB2/1542/ED2696 (pres.B29/1921); LAB2/1899/CEB146 (pres.C5/1925); and also in the *Live Wire*. Minutes of conferences with representatives of ex-servicemen's and women's organisations, 1921–24, are in T162/252/E7061/1 Annexe.

46 When the AWKS held a deputation to the Civil Service Commission on 14 June 1920, to press for equal opportunities and the appointment of a woman deputy commissioner, the Commissioners declared that their department 'was not so important' as the AWKS seemed to think and that they should 'concentrate on more important strategic centres'(!). Moreover, the Commissioners 'strongly supported the women's case; personally they would be overjoyed at the introduction of women into their Department in all grades permanently. BUT the House of Commons, in its recent vote, demanding equality of treatment and pay for women and men Civil Servants, had not defined the Departments which should put this into force, and therefore the vote meant nothing'(!!). One can only assume that the reptilian Sir Stanley Leathes, first Civil Service commissioner, member of the Gladstone Committee, and no friend to women, had his forked tongue tucked firmly in his cheek. 'Deputations: To the Civil Service Commissioners', *Woman Clerk*, 1, 8 (July 1920), p. 87.

47 That is, the Ministry of Food. LAB2/1542/ED2696 (pres. B29/1921), minutes of 18th meeting, 21 January 1921. The AECS's list of August 1923, included the Ministries of Pensions and Labour, the Savings Bank Department of the Post Office and the Air Ministry, a particular *bête noire* with its 'Kingsway Majors' and Royal Aircraft Establishment, Farnborough – RAE: 'Rarely Anyone Enlists'. Argus, 'From My

Rostrum', *Live Wire*, III, 39, pp. 167–8; 'The Farnborough Scandal: A Cuthbert's Paradise', *Live Wire*, II, 28 (September 1922), p. 236.

48 The *Live Wire* pulled no punches. It singled out, for example, Miss Allen, secretary to the Adjutant General to the Forces, a 'lady who has private means, kept on by order of one of Her Majesty's Cabinet Ministers'; 'a certain lady' in the Inland Revenue married to a chief inspector of taxes (salary £1,600 p.a.); and even 'Ladies arriving in motors' (snapshots offered). 'Joint Committee of Ex-Service Men's Unions and Associations (Civil Service), Meeting at Central Hall, Westminster, S.W., Wednesday, 12th January, 1921' [I], 9 (February 1921), p. 23; 'Things the General Secretary Asks' [I], 8 (January 1921), p. 16; 'We Have Heard —' [I], 5 October 1920), p. 14, respectively.

49 POST 33/1866/M13292/1926 Pt. 2, 'Deputation from the Association of Ex-Service Civil Servants received by E. Raven, Esq., . . . on behalf of the Post Master General . . .', 14 December 1926, statement by R. W. Fenn. This deputation is a good illustration of the ex-servicemen's battering ram tactics. In the course of this interview, in addition to the above, the AECS made a general plea for the Post Office to 'adjust matters' so that ex-servicemen could be retained by (1) claiming posts held by temporary women blocking permanent women's appointments in women's departments (the Savings Bank Department, which was perhaps the premier women's department in the Civil Service from the 1870s onwards), and posts (the writing assistant grade); (2) seeking special treatment of 'good competent' men who had failed to make the 'P' grade (see below); (3) touting their 'loyalty' in the General Strike in comparison to women who 'associated themselves with the notorious Anti-Volunteer resolution of the National Whitley Council'; and (4) virtually nominating men to be retained outside the mechanism of the substitution committees. Statements by Mr Hogge and Mr Scott.

50 In this at least they were successful. The Lytton Committee's First [Interim] Report mandated an inquiry into 'the financial position' of all temporary staff, men and women, and the dismissal of 'those found to possess private means', though it did not expect that their numbers would be large (para. 14). The Third [Interim] Report backpedalled: 'We desire, however, to refer to the case of Ex-Service men in possession either of considerable private means or of large service pensions, about whose position particular uncertainty seems to exist. We do not recommend generally that Ex-Service men in receipt of pensions, whether disability or long-service, should be regarded as possessing independent means; but we consider that any such persons possessing private incomes or in receipt of service pensions, which, separately or together, materially exceed the salaries they receive in a civilian capacity, should be liable to substitution'. (para. 11). T162/25/E1634/04 Annexe.

51 T162/24/1634/2, M. G. R[amsay], 'Confidential' memorandum, 18 June 1921.

52 T162/73/E6967, R. R. S[cott], memorandum, 1 October 1921.

53 On the one hand, some members of the Committee deprecated the appointment of ex-servicemen to writing assistant posts, as it would lower efficiency and cause dissatisfaction ('this class of man . . . would become disheartened by the very routine nature of the work') and advocated their employment in 'manipulative and kindred classes'. On the other hand, other members could see 'no adequate reason why this routine work should be refused to the Ex-Service men who are willing to perform it and particularly to those disabled men who are not able freely to compete in the labour market'. T162/25/E1634/04 Annexe, Third [Interim] Report, paras. 51 and 52.

54 T162/98/E11996, H. P[arker], 'Pensions Issue Office Substitution', 4 December 1922. The AECS viewed this honouring of pledges with cynicism: 'The Pensions Minister, who owes his whole department to the war, is, strange to say, the only one who considers himself bound by a pledge . . . a pledge given by one Minister to the women in that Ministry'. 'Broken Pledges', *Live Wire*, II, 18 (November 1921), p. 66.

55 'Awks Branch Notes', *Woman Clerk*, 1, 6 (May 1920), p. 68. Miss Hicks, divisional superintendent in the Soldiers' Awards Branch and a member of the AWKS branch executive, caused quite a stir when she resigned her post, worth £350 a year, in protest at the dismissal/relegation of her colleagues.

56 See T162/252/E7061/1 Annexe, JSB, minutes of liaison meeting, 16 February 1923, and T162/812/E828/2, Parliamentary Question, Erskine, MP, 22 February 1923. The *Live Wire* contains a thrilling account of the doings of the 'Kew Klerks Klan', which began with a work-in and progressed to a lock-out complete with police cordons. Argus, 'From My Rostrum', III, 34 (March 1923), pp. 41–8, 53.

57 T162/25/E1634/04 Annexe, Lytton Committee, First [Interim] Report, para. 17.

58 LAB2/2118/SB451 (pres. A1331), Hilton Young, Treasury, to Macnamara, Labour, 9 November 1920. One year later Sir Russell Scott of the Treasury noted the same thing in exactly the same terms: 'The fact is that there is nothing much left to be substituted . . . in many Departments unquestionably the process of substitution has reached bed rock and further exhortation in these [substitution committee] cases would merely waste time and fray departmental tempers'. T162/252/E7060/1, 3 November 1921.

59 'Who had as a rule little idea of discipline or even decency, and not infrequently were frankly Communistic in their outlook and in their attitude towards the Public and the Post Office'. POST30/4430/E17839/1919 Pt. 45, T. Jardine, London Postal Service, to W. H. Weightman, Secretary's Office, 3 July 1928 ('Not to be circulated outside the Secretary's Office').

60 The Sub-Committee on Temporary Staffs was one of six sub-committees of the National Whitley Council's Reorganisation Committee, and it was – importantly – the only one with a separate independent status. Though the Staff Side was invited to express an opinion, its approval was not required for decisions. That is, although the Committee was created as a result of a Staff Side initiative, the Official Side was in sole control and the Report represented its – i.e., the Treasury's – views and not the joint views of both sides. This was not wholly unconnected with the strong opposition by the men and women of the Staff Side to temporary staffing as an irregular and pernicious form of employment causing blockage of promotion, reduction of mobility, the creation of a pool of low paid and insecure workers who could be used as a weapon against them, the introduction of an alienated group within their midst, and erosion of the good name and high status of the Civil Service. This opposition continued throughout the 1920s and the Staff Side could only complain and offer prognostications of dire consequences, sowing 'the seeds of a long and bitter controversy'. T162/111/14345/2, A. C. Winyard and G. Chase, Staff Side, National Whitley Council, to Stanley Baldwin, 28 March 1925.

61 T162/16/E1035, Civil Service National Whitley Council, Reorganisation Committee, Sub-Committee on Temporary Staffs, Report.

62 T162/812/E828/2, Civil Service notice, August 1920.

63 T162/24/E1634/1, L. C. H. Weekes, Civil Service Commission, to W. R. Fraser, Treasury, 7 September 1920. 18,000 candidates competed for 4,000 places. 'We are not prepared to give details of what we have done in individual cases . . . But I can say that we have pushed up to the qualifying mark a number of disabled men, and have not downgraded any non-disabled to make room for them. It must be remembered that the examination was competitive: we have expended much time and trouble on investigation and have gone far in the direction of leniency'. T162/812/E828/2, Weekes, Civil Service Commission, to J. H. M. Craig, Treasury, 30 August 1921.

64 'Are we to be forced to the conclusion that 75 per cent of those who sat for that test are not competent? . . . There is something wrong! The Examination itself was wrong – the principle of the Examination was wrong'. 'That Examination!', *Live Wire*, II, 13 (June 1921), pp. 1–2. According to the stock letter of complaint sent to MPs the AECS believed that the Treasury had 30,000 posts up its sleeve rather than 4,000 and that it had raised the standard ('higher than in an ordinary Civil Service examination'). These assertions, particularly the latter, irritated the Treasury no end: 'I may say that I have explained the facts to the Secretaries of the Ex-Servicemen's Associations half a dozen times but it does not suit their purpose to accept the explanation, which they never disprove'. T162/812/E828/2, enclosure in J. H. M. Craig, Treasury, to L. C. H. Weekes, Civil Service Commission, 24 August 1921; Hilton Young to H. S. Glanville MP, 27 October 1921, respectively.

65 T162/25/E1634/04 Annexe, Chancellor of the Exchequer's Committee on the Initial Salary of 'Lytton' Entrants and the Appointment of Ex-Service Men to Posts in the Civil Service, Final Report.

66 *Ibid.*, para. 4. And also: '. . . we wish to emphasise the view that the time has now come when definite finality should be given to this question of the employment of ex-service men in the Civil Service. The present uncertainty is disturbing the men and is seriously prejudicial to the efficiency of the Service' (para. 15).

67 Named after Walter Guinness, financial secretary to the Treasury.

68 T162/111/E14345/2, 'Introductory Memorandum No. IX relating to the Employment of Ex-Service Men in the Civil Service', November 1929.

69 T162/334/E28065/080. '. . . it follows that a man had to be a very poor thing indeed not to be able to qualify for the duties normally assigned to temporary clerks'. W. T. Fitzgerald(?), Ministry of Health, to W. T. Matthews, Treasury 29 March 1933.

70 Royal Commission on the Civil Service [hereafter Tomlin Commission], Report (HMSO, 1931), ch. xiv.

71 *Ibid.*, ch. xiv, para. 557.

72 These particular maidens, observed and photographed by the AECS, were 'female writers' (i.e. writing assistants) recruited for the Post Office, aged 15–17 and still wearing their 'school badges on their blazers'. 'Ex-Service Permanent, SBD', 'The Editor's Letter Box: 'Flappers' at Blythe Road SBD', *Live Wire*, III, 41 (October 1923), p. 235.

73 The women's associations, confused, advised their members to sit for both the writing assistant and clerical examinations, even if women had their sights set higher, in order, as it were, to keep their options open. The *Woman Clerk*, for example, while so doing, added encouragingly that the writing assistant grade was 'a class which, if the women civil servants pull together, should ultimately be abolished and absorbed into the clerical grade'. 'Notes on the Forthcoming Civil Service Establishment Examinations', 1, 10 (September, 1920), p. 113. In the same article complaints were voiced that temporary women pensions officers, though given enough time to apply for the examination for local war pensions committee officers (the departmental grade) were given notice nearly too late to apply for the Treasury clerical grades.

74 Pre-war practice was the reverse. For example, writing assistant posts in the Post Office were filled by unsuccessful candidates in the woman clerk examination.

75 E. Miller, 'Secretarial Jottings', *Taxette*, 2, 5 (June 1921), p. 5 and 2, 6 (July 1921), p. 2. Of the 438 successful women, 122 were taxettes, 'our own girls', including the top three.

76 'Of course, the idea of calling it an examination was merely to throw dust in the eyes of the law.' The author was equally scathing about the so-called general knowledge questions, 'super-jazz and ragtime foolery': 'Can anyone, even by the wildest stretch of imagination, being in sound health and of right mind, seriously believe that an exam. which contains [such] questions . . . is a real, genuine, 22-carat, *Civil Service* examination?' Sapiens, 'The Sweepstake', *Taxette*, 1, 10 (November 1920), p. 7.

77 Data is from the following sources (with calculations by the author): P.P. 1919 Cmd. 316 xxxiv 1255–57 and 1926 Cmd 2734 xxi 839–41.

78 T162/111/E14345/2, 'Introductory Memorandum relating to the Employment of Ex-Servicemen in the Civil Service', November 1929, para. 18. Even though the numbers are small, it is interesting to note the distribution of non-service men: the higher the status the higher the percentage – 2·5 per cent in the administrative grade and 2·9 per cent in the Foreign Office and Diplomatic Service; and the lower the status the lower the percentage – 0 per cent in the intermediate grade, 0·2 per cent in the Customs and Excise. This shows that the Treasury was willing to use its discretion when it felt it important to do so.

79 T162/25/E1634/04 Annexe, 'Statement submitted on behalf of the Candidates at the Open Competition . . .' In addition sixteen appointments were made to the Indian Civil Service and the Colonial Civil Service.

80 E. L. Don, 'Joint Substitution Board and Educational Standards', *Live Wire*, II, 13 (June 1921), pp. 7–8.

81 Women were given, confusingly, several choices/combinations of examinations with no indication of how these would pan out in the end: administrative only; administrative with a reversion to executive/higher clerical posts; administrative and executive/higher clerical jointly; executive/higher clerical only; exemption from examination and competitive interview (permanent staff). The great bulk of non-administrative appointments went to women who had taken the administrative examinations only or the administrative/executive/higher clerical examinations jointly. Very few went to those who sat for the executive/higher clerical examination only: '. . . while congratulating the successful ladies, I doubt whether many of them can tell how they came to be favoured'. 'Examination Mystery: The Fee Snatchers of Burlington Gardens: How Women Competitors were Duped: Extraordinary 'Selective' Results', *Live Wire*, III, 33 (February 1923), p. 32, [hereafter 'Examination Mystery'].

82 A practice about which the Federation of Women Civil Servants was very bitter: 'I am directed by my Committee to state that they have a strong objection to permanent women being asked to undergo a further educational test which is not being applied to permanent men'. T162/47/E3506/1, D. Smyth to Ramsay, Treasury, 25 September 1920.

83 'Examination Mystery'.

84 R. K. Kelsall, *Higher Civil Servants in Britain from 1870 to the Present*, London, Routledge and Kegan Paul, 1955, pp. 171, 174.

85 See Table 5.1.

86 T162/289/E27987, 'Posts Reserved to Women', [August 1932].

87 T162/308/E28065/1, National Whitley Council, Temporary Staffs Committee, memorandum, [February 1932]. As of 1 April 1930, 17 per cent of women clerical officers were under 25, 24 per cent were between the ages of 26 and 30, 41 per cent between the ages of 31 and 40; for men these figures were 3 per cent, 18 per cent, and 55 per cent, respectively. (Calculations by the author.)

88 British Library, Gladstone Papers, Add. MS 46,103, fols. 272–3, Emily Penrose, Federation of University Women, to Herbert Gladstone, 29 January 1919.

89 'Examination Mystery'.

6 Rosemary Crompton

The feminisation of the clerical labour force since the Second World War

Introduction

According to the 1981 Census, 74 per cent of 'clerical and related' workers were women; it is the single largest category of women's employment. At the aggregate level, therefore, 'clerical work' (broadly defined) would be judged a segregated, predominantly female occupation (Dex 1985, p. 95ff). In fact, as we shall see in the next section of this paper, the reality is more complex. Extensive segmentation by gender and age exists *within* the 'clerical' category, and it would be mistaken to assume that clerical work is becoming a universally feminine occupation.

Nevertheless, many clerical jobs *are* women's jobs, and this fact is the basic starting point of this paper. The first section will document empirical trends since the Second World War, focussing not only on the feminisation of clerical work, but also on the simultaneous processes of technical change and industrial restructuring. Secondly, the processes of occupational segregation will be explored with a view to illuminating possible sources of change in perceptions of men's and women's social roles – changes which might have far-reaching consequences. Thirdly, the implications of occupational segregation within the clerical category for the current debate on gender and class will be examined.

Occupational segregation – the concentration of men and women in different occupations – has been an important mechanism via which systematic differences in the levels of economic reward between men and women have persisted without violating an ideological commitment to the principles of formal equality. Women are not paid less than men for the same work (this would in any case be illegal), rather, women do different kinds of work, and this work is poorly paid. Given the persistence of occupational segregation, it is argued, equal pay legislation alone is inadequate to achieve the objective of material equalities of reward between the sexes. Hence the Equal Pay (Amendment) Regulations of 1983 allowing employees to claim under the principle of equal pay for work of equal *value*.

It may be further argued that occupational segregation reinforces cultural stereotypes of masculinity and femininity. As Jane Lewis has argued in this volume, 'It is hard to think of jobs that are not gendered'. 'Women's jobs' such as a nurse or receptionist draw upon supposedly feminine attributes and/or overtly female sexuality; lorry drivers and captains of industry, in their different ways, reflect the masculine ideal.

Evidence of the persistence of occupational segregation by gender, therefore, suggests continuity rather than change. Thus although clerical work has been feminised – women now predominate in an occupation in which, fifty years ago, men were a majority – the significance of this gender shift must be evaluated against the fact that probably a majority of male and female clerks do not do the same *jobs*.

Empirical trends

Over the years, the sub-categories of clerical occupations included within the 'clerical and related' category of the census have varied. Although it may be justifiable, therefore, to make inter-censal comparisons of the whole category in order to ascertain broad trends, more detailed comparisons should be made by sub-category in order to ensure that, as far as is possible, like is compared with like. The two

Table 6.1   *The gender composition of the clerical labour force, Great Britain, 1951–81*

	1951	1961	1971	1981
Clerks, cashiers and office machine operators (%)				
Men	51	46	36	30
Women	49	54	64	70
of which (%):				
Married	30	43	57	59
Part-time	6	13	—	25
Total numbers	176,540	231,871	264,098	251,289
Typists, shorthand writers, and secretaries				
(% women)	97	98	99	98
Total numbers	56,680	71,959	77,969	79,106

Source: Census data (10 per cent sample).

major areas of continuity between 1951 and 1981 are firstly: typists, shorthand writers, and secretaries and secondly: clerks, cashiers and office machine operators.[1] (These two groups have comprised between 85 per cent and 100 per cent of the total 'clerical and related' category during the period under discussion).

The first simple point – which cannot, however, be over-emphasised – is that clerical 'feminisation' has occurred in respect of 'clerks and cashiers', and not shorthand writers and secretaries. The latter have been almost totally female occupations since before the Second World War. In 1951, 97 per cent of typists, shorthand writers and secretaries were women, as were 98 per cent in 1981. In contrast, whereas 51 per cent of clerks, cashiers and office machine operators were men in 1951; by 1981 this category was 70 per cent female (Table 6.1).

I have stressed the virtually complete feminisation of typists, shorthand writers and secretaries because of a historical tendency to treat them unproblematically within the clerical category as a whole. Both Lockwood (1958) and Braverman (1974) for example, cite examples drawn from typing and secretarial work in their more general discussion of 'clerks' and the clerical labour process. However, I would suggest that such inclusion is seriously mistaken. As the gender distributions within these 'clerical' sub-categories demonstrate, typing and associated work has long been wholly segregated by gender, whereas clerical work has not. Empirical work has shown that secretarial work is virtually lacking in a career structure which relates to the nature of the work itself. [2] In practice, the secretarial 'career' has been in terms of progressive association with a higher status *boss* (usually male), rather than to officially/explicitly acknowledged positions of power and authority within the organisation. In contrast, for much of the post-war period, clerical work in large bureaucratic organisations could signify the lowest point on a bureaucratic career ladder in theory open to all. In short, to treat typing and clerical jobs as if they unambiguously fell within the same occupational category is *not* to compare like with like.

The proportion of typists, shorthand writers and secretaries relative to other clerical occupations has not varied significantly during the post-war period and, as we have seen, it has remained a virtually female occupation. Further discussion of clerical feminisation will, therefore, deal with the more narrowly defined category of clerks, cashiers, and office machine operators.

Tables 6.2 and 6.3 give details of the age composition of the clerical labour force from 1961 onwards. There has been a relative decline in the proportion of young female clerks, reflecting national trends. From 1961, the age structure of the female clerical labour force has moved closer to that of the national average.

Table 6.3 provides further evidence to demonstrate that increasing numbers of female clerks have been drawn from the older age groups. Indeed, the ratio of male to female clerks in the youngest age category

Table 6.2 *Age profiles of female clerks, cashiers and office machine operators, compared with all economically active women, Great Britain (%)*

		Under 24	25–34	35–44	45–54	55+	Total
1961	Clerks, cashiers, OMO	41	17	18	15	9	100
	Economically active women	29	16	20	21	15	100
1971	Clerks, cashiers, OMO	36	15	17	20	11	100
	Economically active women	25	16	20	22	18	100
1981	Clerks, cashiers, OMO	34	20	18	17	11	100
	Economically active women	24	21	21	20	14	100

Source: Census data.

Table 6.3 *Gender ratio of male and female clerks, cashiers and office machine operators, Great Britain (%)*

	Clerks, cashiers, OMO	Age						*N*
		15–24	25–34	35–44	45–54	55+	Total	(000)
1961	Men	29	49	49	53	67	46	106,763
	Women	71	51	51	47	33	54	125,108
							100	
1971	Men	28	38	32	34	56	36	95,157
	Women	72	62	68	66	44	64	168,941
							100	
1981	Men	26	32	24	27	46	30	74,934
	Women	74	68	76	73	54	70	176,355
							100	

Source: Census data.

has hardly varied at all over the years. In short, the feminisation of the clerical labour force since the Second World War would seem to have involved the substitution of older male clerks by older female clerks.

These changes in the age structure of female clerks, as already noted, reflect changes in women's participation in the labour force which have been extensively documented elsewhere. (Hakim 1979, Martin and Roberts 1984). The increase in women's employment since the

Second World War has been largely an increase in *married* women's employment, particularly women returning to the labour force after domestic breaks for childrearing. Other changes in the structure of the clerical labour force have also followed national trends. In 1961, 30 per cent of all clerks were employed in manufacturing industry, by 1981, this had dropped to 19 per cent. Conversely, Public Administration and Defence employed 11 per cent of all clerks in 1961, but 17 per cent

Table 6.4 *Gender ratios of clerks, cashiers, and office machine operators. Selected industries (Great Britain) (%)*

Industry (1961 = MLH; 1971 = unitgroup; 1981 = industry class)	1961			1971			1981		
	Men	Women	N	Men	Women	N	Men	Women	N
Coal mining	73	27	2,316	65	35	1,488	61	39	1,104
Motor vehicle manufacture	61	39	3,260	58	42	3,676	50	50	2,124
Railways	82	18	6,995	78	22	3,194	74	26	2,331
Education services	14	86	4,429	11	89	7,662	7	93	6,720
Insurance, banking and finance	52	48	25,786	—	—	—	—	—	—
Insurance	—	—	—	38	62	9,728			
Banking – bill-discounting	—	—	—	40	60	19,094	—	—	—
Other financial institutions	—	—	—	38	63	4,332	—	—	—
Insurance (except for compulsory S.S.)	—	—	—	—	—	—	28	72	8,721
Banking finance	—	—	—	—	—	—	33	67	28,742
Total finance	52	48	25,786	39	61	33,154	32	68	37,463
Public admin. and defence	53	47	25,212	38	62	33,542	31	69	42,604

Note: As noted in the text, industrial classifications are not always constant between censuses. The area between the dotted lines, therefore, gives the relevant data for the finance industries for the census year in question; aggregate information is given in the 'Total finance' row.

Source: Census Data.

by 1981, and other services (including financial services) employed 26 per cent in 1961, but 38 per cent by 1981. (Transport, Distribution and a residual 'other' category have been omitted from these comparisons).

These shifts, of course, reflect the decline of manufacturing employment in Britain during this period, together with the substantial rise in service employment.

More detailed investigation also reveals interesting concentrations by industry. For example, although in 1961 male clerks (52 per cent) predominated over female clerks (48 per cent) in the manufacturing industry as a whole, female clerks (62 per cent) were in the majority in textiles, an industry with a high proportion of female employees. Conversely, although clerical employment in manufacturing was 67 per cent female by 1981, male clerks still predominated in coal mining. (Table 6.4).

Of rather more interest, however, are the changes which have occurred within the service sector. In 1961, male clerks were still in the majority in the great bureaucracies of finance and the public sector, but by 1981 these areas of clerical employment had expanded and feminised. In contrast, sectors providing disproportionately more male clerical employment, such as manufacturing and transport, have declined. Changes in Industrial Classification make inter-censal comparisons problematic. However, Table 6.4 illustrates these trends using industrial groups for which comparisons are possible.

Changes in the structure of clerical employment, therefore, reflect both the increasing participation of women in the waged work as well as other developments in the economy. However, other significant changes were also occurring, notably the rationalisation and computerisation of the white-collar labour process, and changes in social attitudes towards women and women's work associated with the growth of neo-feminism.[3]

Deskilling and the feminisation of clerical work

Office work has been subject to routinisation and deskilling from the beginnings of the emergence of large bureaucracies (Lowe 1988, Cohn 1986, Crompton and Jones 1984, Chapter 2). As Braverman (1974) emphasises, early protagonists of Taylorism or 'Scientific Management' were as anxious to apply the principles of their 'science' to office work as to work in manufacturing industry. However, although the physical aspects of clerical work could be subjected to time and motion study (for example, number of characters typed per minute), and simple tasks measured (for example, sorting, filing), much clerical work involved the manipulation and transmission of knowledge which, until comparatively recently, was elusive to control. It is this previous dimension of clerical work that led Braverman to suggest historic parallels with craft work, and Lockwood (1958) to suggest that 'In the large firm, as in the small, much clerical work is specific, non-repetitive, requiring a modicum of skill and responsibility and individual judgement'. (p. 78).

The introduction of computers, however, facilitated massive changes. Not least among these was the fact that their effective utilisation (particularly in the early years when batch systems predominated), involved the breaking down of non-manual processes such as payroll, insurance claims, cheque clearing, client records and so on into a series of routine operations. There has been an extended debate as to whether the net effect of computer-related change will be to 'upgrade' (i.e. reskill) or 'downgrade' (i.e. deskill) the labour force as a whole, whether the introduction of computerised systems will make routine work a thing of the past or conversely, increase the number of routine jobs. This is not a central topic of this paper but it may be argued that whatever has been the fate of the *individuals* concerned, it is indisputable that many clerical *procedures* have been routinised. Thus much of the work associated with these routine procedures, particularly the coding and inputting of data, *is* routine work.[4]

These changes, not surprisingly, were accompanied by the re-structuring of the clerical labour force. As has been described elsewhere:

In the United Kingdom commercial computers were first introduced in the late 1950s and early 1960s, and subsequent expansion has been rapid. By 1965, the Prices and Incomes Board described the impact on bank work – as follows: 'the nature of banking is changing . . . much of the routine work has been mechanised and the use of computers is growing . . . This change in the nature of banking has been accompanied by a change in the kind of staff required (NBPI Report 6, p. 14). Different kinds of employees, the PIB suggested, were required for the routine, computerised work, in contrast to the relatively small number of 'career' staff who would henceforth be needed. (Crompton and Jones 1984, p. 43).

The introduction of computers to facilitate the work of large white-collar bureaucracies occurred during a period of rapid expansion of business. During previous research into white-collar work (Crompton and Jones 1984), we were frequently assured that the introduction of computers was simply essential in order to cope with the increasing volume of activity in the financial sector. These decades (the 1950s, 60s, and 70s) were also, of course, a period of very rapid growth of national and local government employment associated with the expansion of the welfare state and other services such as health and education. Although, therefore, computerisation eventually led to labour savings, the period of their introduction was nevertheless one of expanding demand for clerical labour. (Table 6.1).

The demand for clerical labour was therefore rising at the same time as the clerical labour process was becoming increasingly routinised. However, labour was readily available as married women re-entered the labour force in ever increasing numbers. (Hakim 1979, Martin and Roberts 1984). The phenomenon of women being hired to carry out routine clerical work lacking in promotion prospects is almost as old as clerical work itself. (Cohn 1986, Davies 1974). Cohn has coined the phrase 'synthetic turnover' to describe the inter-war situation in Britain. He describes how, in the Post Office and Great Western Railway, women were hired either in 'women only' grades and/or subjected to marriage bars – that is, the formal requirement that they resign, or move to non-career grades, on marriage. The 'synthetic turnover' thus induced ensured a constant supply of low-level clerical labour with few career prospects.

One interpretation of the change in the age profiles of the female clerical labour force described in Tables 6.2 and 6.3 is that, to adapt Cohn's phrase, 'synthetic turnover' has been augmented by 'synthetic immobility'. Young women are recruited into lower clerical grades but, as the Women and Employment survey has demonstrated, they have tended to leave the full-time labour force during the family formation phase although they may (increasingly) engage in inter- mittent employment and part-time work. (Dex 1984). When they return to work after a child-rearing break, they are effectively unpromotable (hence 'synthetic immobility'); not only because of the career break but also because, perhaps in anticipation of it, many will not have acquired the formal qualifications associated with linear careers, or be available for overtime working or geographic mobility. More detailed examination of age breakdowns, however, suggests that this explanation may be too simple.

Table 6.5 gives age profiles of male and female clerks, by selected industries, for 1981. It is immediately apparent that there are very considerable variations by industry, suggesting that quite different elements of the clerical labour 'pool' are being tapped by different employers. The data in Table 6.5 will be used in part to summarise what is already known, and in part to develop further the account of segmentation within the clerical category.

Table 6.5 *Age profiles of Male and Female Clerks, selected industries, 1981 (% by row)*

Industry class		Up to 24	25–34	35–44	45–54	55+	N (10% sample)
	Women						
35	Motor vehicles	28	20	23	20	9	921
32	Mechanical engineering	31	18	19	21	11	3,917
79	Postal services	29	17	15	21	18	4,549
81	Banking and finance	57	22	10	8	3	18,636
82	Insurance, except compulsory social security	50	16	12	14	8	5,886
91	Public admin. and national defence	32	21	16	17	13	28,001
93	Education	10	12	29	32	17	6,061
	All women clerks (total industry classes)	33	20	18	18	11	164,967
	Men						
35	Motor vehicles	12	20	17	26	24	1,008
32	Mechanical engineering	16	20	15	21	28	2,387
79	Postal services	28	23	13	17	19	2,287
81	Banking and finance	43	27	13	10	7	9,125
82	Insurance, except compulsory social security	49	18	9	10	14	2,390
91	Public admin. and national defence	28	21	11	15	25	12,966
93	Education	21	19	13	20	27	426
	All male clerks (total industry classes)	27	22	13	16	23	72,013

Note: Only clerks (occupational group 046) are included in this table. Note also that totals are given for the purpose of comparison, and not as the sum of the table.

Firstly, the age profile of male clerks is double-peaked. The second peak, as Stewart *et al.* (1980) have noted, represents the recruitment of older men, often ex-manual workers, to the clerical labour force. However, inter-industry comparisons reveal that the second peak is particularly marked in manufacturing industry, and the bimodal pattern present in only public administration and the postal services amongst the industries illustrated. (The former, we have argued, reflects the long-standing practice in manufacturing of placing long-service employees in lower-level white-collar jobs, Crompton and

Jones (1984)). However, in the finance industries the relative lack of older male clerks is striking and the 'bimodal' pattern virtually absent. The financial bureaucracies are characterised by formal job hierarchies (or internal labour markets) through which the majority of young men recruited as clerks have historically progressed; thus the absence of older male clerks. Formal job hierarchies are also a feature of public service bureaucracies, but case study evidence suggests that such public service (and public spirited?) organisations are also more likely to provide jobs for older men without orthodox 'white-collar' backgrounds. (Crompton and Jones *op. cit.*, p. 121).[5]

The variations in the age profiles of the female clerks are also considerable. Averaged data (see also Table 6.2) suggests that clerical work is more likely to be a younger woman's occupation. However, the data by industry in Table 6.5 suggests that some areas of clerical work are largely populated by older women. The most striking contrast is between female clerks in the finance sector as compared with education. Half of the women clerks in insurance and banking are under twenty-five; half of the women clerks in education are over forty-five. (More women clerks are employed in education (60,610) than in insurance (58,860)).

These contrasts are not difficult to explain. Rather as school-teaching is an eminently 'suitable' job for a professional woman, (Crompton and Sanderson 1987), so a job as a clerk in education – say a school secretary – is an eminently 'suitable' job for a woman clerk, *particularly* a woman with children still at school. More than three-quarters of women clerks in education are over thirty-five; I would suggest that the vast majority of these women will have brought up, or be bringing up, children themselves – gaining 'domestic sphere' skills and experience which will be invaluable – although unlikely to be financially acknowledged – in their 'public sphere' work.[6]

The more detailed comparisons by age, therefore, suggest that we should make some slight modifications to the argument developed earlier. Older women clerks (like older male clerks), are very unlikely to be promoted because of their alleged deficiencies in 'human capital' – broken careers, lack of job related qualifications, etc. They thus present little threat to the male clerical career, rather like earlier generations of young female clerks faced with women-only grade structures and marriage bars. Until comparatively recently, contemporary young women clerks – despite the removal of institutional barriers to formal equality of opportunity – appear to have removed

themselves from career competition with men on the advent of family
responsibilities. They have in practice not been promoted, although in
theory promotable. However, although younger and older female
clerical labour apparently shares similar characteristics in respect of *de
facto* organisational immobility; the evidence of Table 6.5 suggests that
younger and older women clerks tend to do rather *different* types of
work. It is perhaps misleading, therefore, to describe older female
clerical labour as 'augmenting' that of younger, as in many cases they
do not do similar jobs. Although considerable over-generalisation is
involved, it may be suggested that whereas young women have been
recruited in increasing numbers to undertake the routine, deskilled
work associated with the computerisation of the clerical labour
process, older women have more frequently been employed to carry
out the lower-level administration and 'people work' associated with
the expansion of public and private services.

Implications of occupational segregation

Sources of social change
The evidence reviewed so far in this paper reveals considerable
segmentation by gender and age within clerical employment. In the
great expansion of clerical work for women many jobs have been
constructed as culturally gendered occupations; as 'women's work' or
'men's work'. However, although both the persistence of occupational
segregation and cultural ideas about 'proper' gender roles may be
constants, they are *not* immutable (Davidoff 1986). Notions of 'correct'
behaviour – and following from this, 'correct' employment – for men
and women vary not only over time but also between different strata of
society.

Post-war developments in Britain have, indeed, seen considerable
changes in ideas relating to masculinity and femininity. Under the
pressure of neo-feminism, women have acquired more of the attributes
of 'social citizenship', that is, the acquisition of civil, political and
welfare rights which are the property of all 'citizens' (Marshall 1951).
Equal Pay and Anti-Discrimination legislation (1970, 1975) has
bestowed a formal, legal equality on women and men doing the same
kind of work.

The feminism which has contributed to legislative changes has, of
course, had an impact beyond this, particularly as far as the shaping of
attitudes is concerned. Although the importance of 'second wave'

feminism in finally securing legislation has been emphasised above, it would probably be true to suggest that overt and legal discrimination against women on the grounds of their sex would in any case eventually have been eroded given the continuing adherence to the ideology of bourgeois liberalism in the West (Eisenstein 1981). More insidious in their effects, it might be argued, have been ideas of masculinity and femininity which effectively place women in an inferior position despite protestations of sexual equality. Since the 1960s, however, feminists have made it one of their major tasks to challenge such assumptions. In particular, there has been a re-evaluation of child-care practices and maternal responsibilities. (New and David 1985).

Central to the construction of femininity is the woman's actual or anticipated role as a wife and mother. Historically mothers have usually assumed the prime responsibility for the care of young children. Whether this is a consequence of biological dependence, as Brenner and Ramas (1984) have argued, or whether this provides yet more evidence for patriarchal repression, as radical feminists might suggest, is immaterial to this argument. However, ideas about the 'proper' rearing of young children have been subject to enormous swings of fashion, from the rigid schedules of absence of physical contact advocated by Truby King, to the more permissive regimes of the 1960s. It is probably true that the practical reality of childrearing has always owed more to parental instincts and preferences than textbook knowledge, but, perhaps paradoxically, 'scientific' theories of the child and mother are more likely to have had an impact on official policy than commonsense practice.

During the Second World War, women, including the mothers of young children, were taken into the labour force and a network of state provision for young children created. However, after the war, as Riley (1983) has argued, the combination of universal post-war pronatalism and the popular dissemination of Bowlby's work was 'deadly'. As a Kleinian-influenced social psychologist, Bowlby (1952, 1953) argued that the nature of the mother-child bond was central to the mental health of the future adult. His work was widely interpreted to mean that *any* separation of mother and child was potentially damaging. For example, a 1958 pamphlet entitled 'Can I leave my baby?' implied that, apart from the possibility of a brief shopping trip, the answer was 'No' (*ibid* p. 10).

The immediate post-war period, therefore, was one in which, it may be argued, the 'messages' being received by women regarding employment were potentially contradictory. The post-war economy was booming and demand for labour increasing. Moves were being made towards a formal equality of treatment in the workplace through the removal of marriage bars etc. (Whitley Council 1946) and moves toward equal pay. On the other hand, mothers were being repeatedly told that their real 'work' lay at home in caring for their children. As Riley (1983, p. 188) has succinctly expressed it: '. . . women were, rhetorically, both over-personified as mothers and desexed as workers'. A solution to this contradiction was achieved in the events which followed. Married women *did* return to the labour force, but increasingly as part-time workers and usually after having partially completed their 'real' work – the rearing of children. (Wilson 1980).

The fiction that women were 'sexless' in the labour force was nevertheless further reinforced by the passing of equal pay and opportunities legislation. However, as we have seen in the evidence reviewed in this paper, the fact of occupational segregation by gender belies the fiction. Women do not enter the labour force as un-differentiated labour, but as potential or actual wives and mothers. The work they do is often a reflection of this as well as other aspects of the feminine role.

Occupational segregation by sex, it has been argued in the introduction to this paper, is of considerable significance in main-taining the status quo as far as men and women are concerned. If men and women do different kinds of work, then women may continue to receive lower rates of pay even if equal pay legislation is enforced. Women's resentment at lack of promotion prospects is lower if they are confined to all-female ghettoes where 'fast track' men are absent. (Crompton and Jones 1984). In short, occupational segregation neatly solves the problem of maintaining the distinction between male and female in a domain – the public realm – where the untramelled, asexual 'individual' is supposedly sovereign.

The solution, however, is unstable. Although the extent of gender segregation within the clerical category has been stressed in this paper it is by no means complete. Some clerical jobs – typing, key-punching, secretarial work – are virtually 100 per cent female and some employment sectors – notably education – likewise; but many women, as we found in our research, work in the same jobs as men. In particular, women recruited into financial and public service bureau-cracies have been, since the early 1960s, initially placed in the same grade structure as men. (These are, as demonstrated in Table 6.4, the fastest growing areas of clerical employment). The evidence of Table 6.5 suggests that, until comparatively recently, a substantial proportion of the young women recruited to these lower level clerical jobs have left at a relatively young age – i.e. even though formal marriage bars have been removed, expectations of motherhood have had a similar effect. It may be argued that this merely further demonstrates the enduring nature of gendered inequality. If the outcome – women staying in lower level jobs – is the same whether they are recruited to specifically 'women's jobs' or fail to achieve movement from 'unisex' lower level jobs then does a difference in the processes underlying the result really matter?

On the other hand, it may be argued, that such 'vertical segregation by exclusion' – i.e. the recruitment of men and women to similar jobs, but the subsequent promotion of men, rather than women – is likely to lead to tensions because of its very 'transparency'.[7] In empirical research carried out in the early 1980s, resentment was found to be widespread, particularly amongst the younger women, at their failure to be promoted as compared to young men doing the same kind of work. The ideology of equal rights and opportunities may be effectively short-circuited if men and women are recruited to *different* jobs; if, however, they are not, then there will emerge pressure for practice to measure up to ideological prescription.

Subsequent empirical work (Crompton and Sanderson 1986, 1987) suggests that increasing numbers of young women are acquiring job-related qualifications (which they had not done hitherto) essential to the pursuit of organisational careers. It is not being suggested that the proportion of promoted female clerks will automatically increase – there are many historical instances of well-educated young women being effectively confined to lowly occupations (Davies 1974). However, this time there is a significant difference in the context – discrimination by sex is illegal and the qualifications being obtained are universally applicable. Just as important, perhaps, is the change in perceptions of appropriate roles of men and women. Women still carry the major burden of childcare, but the excessively child-centred mother of the 1950s and 1960s is no longer held up as the ideal. Maternity leave provision has officially placed a return to work on the agenda, even though most women may not, in fact, take advantage of it. (What evidence there is, however, suggests that take-up rates are higher amongst qualified women). The kinds of pressures which produced, almost universally, broken careers (or rather, work experience) for women in the 1950s and 1960s are at least receding.

It has been argued, therefore, that a number of related changes have occurred in respect of ideas relating to femininity, and women's roles as wives and mothers, which may have an even greater impact on future generations of women. The formal principles of liberal individualism have been reasserted and codified in law. It is not too fanciful to suggest that in the 'moral climate' which followed from the atrocities of the Second World War, and the emergent conflict of ideologies in the 'cold war', this reassertion was hardly surprising. Secondly, the growth of feminism since the 1960s has radically challenged 'conventional' assumptions about women, wives, and mothers. It is unlikely that anything approaching a total transformation has occurred, but certainly attitudinal evidence, together with evidence of the increased rate of acquisition of 'career' qualifications by women, (Crompton and Sanderson 1986) suggests that young women in the 1970s and 1980s, in contrast to those in the 1930s and even 1950s, are not as content to dwell in the feminised ghettoes of the occupational structure.

Finally, changing patterns of occupational segregation may be used to explore possible sources of cultural change. In the debates on 'gender and class', (where 'class' is interpreted as location in the occupational structure: Brenner and Ramas 1984, Barrett 1984, Lewis 1985), a contrast between 'ideological' and 'economistic' explanations of women's place has often been sharply drawn. A preferable approach would recognise the interaction between the two. For example, an 'economistic' argument might be developed that the growth of second wave feminism followed on from women's increased participation in the formal economy after the Second World War. Alternatively, an 'ideological' argument might be suggested; that a renewed emphasis on feminism was an 'outcome' of the enhanced significance of individualism in the post-war period. Both of these approaches over-simplify. It is more useful to recognise that the structure of employment is itself 'gendered' – although not universally. Some jobs, therefore, will tend to reinforce per-ceptions of the proper feminine role, particularly those involving nurture, caring, or an overt display of feminine sexuality – Recep-tionist, clerk-typist in a primary school, etc. Thus, participation in waged work will reinforce, rather than challenge, feminine stereotypes. Other jobs, however, – for example, bank clerk, local government clerk in a large office – will be more gender neutral. In these cases, not only will the feminine role not be significantly enhanced, but the different experiences of young men in similar jobs might serve to sharpen the negative comparisons between men's and women's career fates. Such experiences of relative deprivation, it may be suggested, might well be a source of changing ideas. Thus the experience of work might either reinforce or undermine the ideology of femininity.

A parallel argument might be developed concerning the relationship between the 'public' and private or domestic spheres and their impact on work in both. It has been argued that the conflict between an ideology of equality and the experience of inequality in *employment* might be a source of ideological change (Eisenstein 1981) and indeed, as has been indicated above, there are likely to be instances where this *is* the case. However, it could also be suggested that the increasing and explicit identification of women's identity with the home in the 1950s and early 1960s, despite protestations of formal equality, was even more important in changing women's perceptions than their 'public sphere' experiences. (Friedan 1975, Gavron 1968). The family, that 'haven in a heartless world' may, it has been demonstrated, be an area of stress and deprivation for women. (Brown *et al.* 1975).

The debate on class and gender

The significance of 'the clerk' to sociological debate lies in the fact that since the beginnings of occupational classifications, it has been placed at the point of the hierarchical divide, at the lowest level of the 'non-manual' hierarchy which itself embodies 'management'. Thus Lockwood: 'Because of the rigid division between the 'office' and the 'works' it is no exaggeration to say that 'management', from the point of view of the manual worker, ends with the lowest grade of routine clerk' (1958, p. 81). However, from before and increasingly since the Second World War, the clerical 'labour process' (to use the term loosely) has been increasingly routinised and fragmented and in 1974 Braverman asserted that

The problem of the so-called employee or white-collar worker which so bothered early generations of Marxists, and which was hailed by anti-Marxists as proof of the falsity of the 'proletarianization' thesis, has thus been unambiguously clarified by the polarization of office employment and the growth at one pole of an immense mass of wage workers. (*ibid* p. 355).

Following conventional practice, women clerks have been allocated to the same occupational category as male clerks – as indeed are male and female teachers, security guards, postmen (*sic*) or whatever. However, it is doubtful whether the majority of female clerks have *ever* been regarded as possessing 'managerial' status – even if this is or has been true of male clerks.

In common with other authors, Lockwood treated men as the major agents in the class structure. His theoretical framework distinguished three elements which together comprised 'class situation' – these were work situation, market situation, and status situation.[8] Women were viewed as enhancing the market situation of the male clerk in that their concentration in the lower ranks improved men's promotion prospects, (p. 68); and also as positively contributing to men's work situation in that it was largely women who carried out the routine mechanised tasks (p. 92). Women's contribution to the status situation of the male clerk, however, was negative, as the association with 'women's work' 'stigmatised' clerical labour. (pp. 122–125).

Whilst it is certainly not the case, therefore, that Lockwood ignored clerical feminisation, its significance was discussed almost entirely in relation to the impact of the presence of female clerks on the male clerks' 'life-chances' and social standing, rather than as a phenomenon worthy of consideration in its own right. In 'mainstream' sociological stratification theory and research, this approach still predominates. For example, Giddens (1973) described women as 'the "underclass" of the white-collar sector' (p. 288), and in a more recent (and trenchant) statement, Goldthorpe (1983) has reasserted the 'conventional view' that a woman's occupational (or class) status is 'overdetermined by that of her husband'; echoing Lockwood's comments on '. . . the routine girl clerk or typist of the modern office, whose future status depends less on her own career than on that of the man she ultimately marries.' (*ibid* p. 125).

However, this apparent anomaly – i.e. that the occupation of what is ostensibly a similar position in 'the social division of labour' (Goldthorpe 1983) has very different consequences depending upon the gender of the occupant – has contributed to a number of different arguments. Goldthorpe, as already noted, has used it to support his argument that the 'class structure' can be effectively studied by examining only male employment. His critics (Stanworth 1984, Heath and Britten 1984) have argued for the growing significance of the 'cross-class' family and female employment more generally. Stewart *et al.* (1980) have focused upon the diversity of experience within the 'clerical' category in order to support their broader argument (*contra-*Goldthorpe) concerning the utility of the occupational structure in measures of social stratification.

As we have seen, the actual situation is so complex that aspects of it could be used to give partial support to a range of theoretical positions. Gender segregation within clerical work *is* extensive and most young men entering clerical work *will* be promoted or leave. (Stewart, Prandy, Blackburn). The clerical labour process *has* been deskilled and an 'immense mass of wage workers' now perform clerical tasks (Braverman). The extent of gender segregation *does* lend plausibility to arguments that women are a white-collar 'underclass', and/or a 'buffer zone' in the occupational structure (Giddens, Mann 1986). The subordinate position of women in the 'public sphere' *could* be used in support of arguments that the 'life chances' (or class situation) of married women are dependent on that of their husbands and, therefore, the 'class structure' may be investigated via men only (Goldthorpe).

However, I would argue that *all* of these accounts are partial, and therefore, potentially misleading. The persistence of gender segregation should not, as it so often has done, provide the rationale for focusing on men's jobs alone. It would have been equally mistaken to focus on women's jobs. Rather, it should be stressed that the division of labour is *itself* gendered. To adapt Stacey's (1981) oft-quoted insight, it is *not* that there are two divisions of labour, 'one that it all began with Adam Smith and the other that it all began with Adam and Eve' – rather there is *one* division of labour, which is stratified by gender.

Occupational segregation, it has been argued, may be (crudely) viewed as an arrangement whereby the lower cultural (and therefore material) 'worth' of women is accommodated whilst the ideological principle of equality is maintained. If women choose to do different jobs to men, and if these jobs happen to pay less, why not? Although the jobs that women do have lower returns than those of men, a man doing the *same* job would, since 1975 at any rate, get the same rate of pay. Once occupational segregation *is* explicitly acknowledged, then it can be seen that the status of a particular job does *not* depend on the status (or gender) of the *individual* occupant, and Lockwood is correct to argue that 'it is the position of an occupation within some hierarchy of authority that is decisive for its status and not the sex of the person who happens to be in it'. (1986, p. 21).

However, although this argument is valid as far as the individual is concerned, the status of an occupation *is* affected by whether it is 'male' or 'female', as well as other factors such as, for example, educational requirements. If it is important to stress the significance of occupational segregation, then it is *equally* important to stress that it is far from universal. If it were, then the empirical and conceptual problems which have beset stratification research and theory could be solved. Jobs in the occupational hierarchy could simply be labelled 'male' or 'female' and the hierarchy disaggregated when required. As we have seen in our examination of clerical occupations, some jobs – for example, typing and secretarial work – are so thoroughly feminised that the stratagem of developing separate male and female occupational hierarchies might initially appear feasible. However, clerical work also provides examples – for example, bank clerks, local authority clerks – where segregation is far from complete. Women may be confined to lower level positions in these hierarches, but they are *kept* there by the application of exclusionary rules. It should also be noted that, since the passing of the sex discrimination act, women cannot formally be barred from traditionally male preserves to which they had previously not been recruited. (See, for example, the EOC (1985) report on the Leeds Permanent). As long as an ideology of equal opportunity persists, segregation by exclusion will be unstable.

As we have seen, ideologies of formal equality may for extended periods be counterbalanced by cultural prescriptions relating to masculinity and feminity. Once these are challenged, however, the situation becomes unstable. Following from this, it may be argued that it is not necessary to resolve whether 'class first' or 'patriarchy first' arguments are the more valid (Sargent 1981). It *is* necessary to recognise, however, that classes are gendered. Marx did not, Weber did not, neither have successive generations of class theorists – but this should not be a barrier to belated recognition. It is not necessary to abandon class theory, but it is necessary to recognise that the 'class structure' is sustained by gender relationships as well as relations of economic exploitation. Shifts in gender relationships and related conflict may have a *more* important impact on society as far as the short run is concerned, and who can predict the long?

Notes

This essay has also been given as a faculty seminar paper at the Universities of Kent and Edinburgh, and I would like to acknowledge the comments of the participants. Leonore

Davidoff, David Lockwood, Gordon Marshall and Jane Lewis have all commented on earlier drafts. The outcome also owes much to conversations with Kay Sanderson.

1 It may be objected – and I would have to agree – that the two categories I have adopted for the purposes of longitudinal comparison are themselves not consistent. The occupation of 'secretary', for example, carries with it considerably more prestige and pay than 'typist'. However, they have been aggregated from 1961 onwards. 'Office machine operators' (rather less than 10% of the combined category) should probably not be included with clerks, but their aggregation in the 1961 census makes it necessary to combine them for other years for the purposes of comparison.

2 Downing's (1981) work, for example, suggests that the status order amongst secretaries has as much association with family background, etc., as the work they do. See also McNally (1979).

3 The terms 'neo' and 'second wave' feminism will be used to refer to the renewed attention to and impact of feminist thinking which developed in Britain and elsewhere from the late 1960s. It may be argued that some of my earlier work (1976, 1979) did not pay sufficient attention to gender, and I would agree.

4 It may be argued that routine work may nevertheless be of great complexity, requiring a high level of skill (for example, an airline pilot). The concept of 'skill' raises a number of difficult problems centring on 'social' and 'technical' aspects of the phenomenon (Crompton 1987). However, the empirical research cited as evidence (Crompton and Jones 1984) demonstrated that significant control was largely absent from most routine white-collar jobs. Certainly the work tasks we investigated were not particularly complex either. It may be suggested that more recent technological developments incorporating interactive terminals *may* increase the complexity of clerical operations, but for the moment the case remains not proven.

5 Further evidence which suggests that relatively 'disadvantaged' workers are more likely to gain employment in the public sector is provided by the fact that the proportion of registered disabled employed is also higher.

6 During previous fieldwork, we came across examples of older, mature women acting as 'clerks in charge' of local authority field units such as day centres for the handicapped. (Crompton and Jones, p. 146). The tasks involved are similar to those carried out by school secretaries, and draw upon 'caring' as well as technic 1 skills. Given the nature of public service and local government activity, such niches for older women are more likely to be available there than in the finance sector, where customers 'like to see a pretty face behind the counter', (*ibid.* p. 258). Both the finance and public service sector are characterised by internal labour markets, but a further characteristic of public service employment would appear to be these static niches for *older* women, which would explain the difference in the female age profiles between these two major areas of 'service' employment. Comparisons with the age profiles of typists etc. suggests that many older women clerks have trained as typists and secretaries during their first employment phase – but the longitudinal data needed to demonstrate this point is not available.

7 Milkman (1983) makes a similar point in her historical account of 'male' and 'female' jobs in electrical assembly. 'Women's jobs' were supposedly 'lighter', but their basic similarity to those of the men made gender differences difficult to justify.

8 'Under "class position" will be included the following factors. First "market situation", that is to say the economic position narrowly conceived, consisting of source and size of income, degree of job-security, and opportunity for upward occupational mobility. Secondly, "work situation", the set of social relationships in which the individual is involved at work by virtue of his position in the division of labour. And finally, "status situation", or the position of the individual in the hierarchy of prestige in the society at large.' (Lockwood 1958, p. 15).

Bibliography

Barrett, M. (1984) 'Rethinking women's oppression: a reply to Brenner and Ramas', *New Left Review*, No. 146 (July–August).

Bowlby, J. (1952) *Maternal Care and Mental Health*, WHO, Geneva.

Bowlby, J. (1953 and 1965) *Child Care and the Growth of Love*, Penguin, Harmondsworth.

Braverman, H. (1974) *Labour and Monopoly Capital*, Monthly Review Press, New York.

Brenner, J. and Ramas, M. (1984) 'Rethinking Women's Oppression', *New Left Review*, No. 144, pp. 33–71.

Brown, G. W., Bhrolchain, M. N. and Harris, T., (1975) 'Social Class and Psychiatric Disturbance among Women in an Urban Population', *Sociology* Vol. 9, pp. 225–53.

Cohn, S. (1986) *The Process of Occupational Sex-Typing*, Temple, Philadelphia.

Crompton, R. (1976) 'Approaches to the Study of White-Collar Unionism', *Sociology*, Vol. 10, No. 3 (September).

Crompton, R. (1979) 'Trade Unionism and the Insurance Clerk', *Sociology* Vol. 13 (September).

Crompton, R. and Jones, G (1984), *White-Collar Proletariat: Deskilling and Gender in the Clerical Labour Process*, Macmillan, London.

Crompton, R. and Sanderson, K. (1986), 'Credentials and Careers: Some Implications of the Increase in Professional Qualifications amongst Women', *Sociology*, Vol. 20, No. 1.

Crompton, R. and Sanderson, K. (1987), 'Where did all the bright girls go?', *Quarterly Journal of Social Affairs* (April).

Davidoff, L. (1986) 'The Role of Gender in the First Industrial Nation' in Crompton, R. and Mann, M. (eds.), *Gender and Stratification*, Polity, Cambridge.

Davies, M. (1974), 'Women's Place is at the Typewriter: the Feminization of the Clerical Labour Force', *Radical America*, Vol. 8, No. 4.

Dex, S. (1984), *Women's Work Histories: an Analysis of the Women and Employment Survey*, Research Paper No. 46, Department of Employment.

Downing, H. (1981), 'Developments in Secretarial Labour: Resistance, Office Automation and the Transformation of Patriarchal Relations of Control', PhD, University of Birmingham.

Eisenstein, Z. (1981), *The Radical Future of Liberal Feminism*, New York, Longman.

Freidan, B. (1975), *The Feminine Mystique*, Penguin, Harmondsworth.

Gavron, H. (1968), *The Captive Wife*, Penguin, Harmondsworth.

Giddens, A. (1973 and 1981) *The Class Structure of the Advanced Societies*, Hutchinson, London.

Goldthorpe, J. H., Lockwood, D., Bechofer, F. and Platt, J. (1969), *The Affluent Worker in the Class Structure*, Cambridge University Press.

Goldthorpe, J. H., with Llewellyn, C. and Payne, C. (1980), *Social Mobility and Class Structure in Modern Britain*, Clarendon Press, Oxford.

Goldthorpe, J. H. (1983) 'Women and Class Analysis: In Defence of the Conventional View', *Sociology*, Vol. 17, No. 4 (November).

Hakim, C. (1979), *Occupational Segregation*, D. E. Research Paper No. 9 (November).

Hartmann, H. I. (1981), 'The Unhappy Marriage of Marxism and Feminism: Towards a More Progressive Union' in Sargent, L. (ed.), *Women and Revolution*, Boston, South End Press.

Heath, A. and Britten, N. (1984), 'Women's Jobs Do Make a Difference', *Sociology*, Vol. 18, No. 4 (November).

Lewis, J. (1985), 'The Debate on Sex and Class', *New Left Review*, No. 149 (January/February).

Lockwood, D. (1958), *The Blackcoated Worker*, George Allen and Unwin, London.

Lockwood, D. (1986), 'Class, Status and Gender' in Crompton, R. and Mann, M. (eds.) *Gender and Stratification*, Polity, Cambridge.

Lowe, G. S. (1987), *The Feminization of Clerical Work: Women and the Administrative Revolution in Canada*, 1901–31, Polity, Cambridge.

McNally, F. (1979), *Women for Hire: a study of the female office worker*, London, Macmillan.

Mann, M. (1986), 'A Crisis in Stratification Theory' in Crompton, R. and Mann, M. (eds.), *Gender and Stratification*, Polity, Cambridge.

Marshall, T. H. (1951), 'Citizenship and Social Class' in Marshall, T. H., *Sociology at the Crossroads*, Tavistock, London.

Martin, J. and Roberts, C. (1984), *Women and Employment: A Lifetime Perspective*, HMSO.

Milkman, R. (1983) 'Female Factory Labour and Industrial Structure: Control and Conflict over 'Women's place' in Auto and Electrical Manufacturing', *Politics and Society*, pp. 159–203.

New, C. and David, M. (1985), *For the Children's Sake*, Penguin, Harmondsworth.

Riley, D. (1983), *War in the Nursery: Theories of the Child and Mother*, Virago, London.

Sargent, L. (ed.) (1981), *Women and Revolution*, Boston, South End Press.

Stacey, M. (1981), 'The Division of Labour Revisited or Overcoming the Two Adams', *Practice and Progress: British Sociology 1950–1980* ed. P. Abrams *et al.*, George Allen and Unwin, London.

Stanworth, M. (1984), 'Women and class analysis: a reply to John Goldthorpe', *Sociology*, Vol. 18, No. 2.

Stewart, A., Prandy, K. and Blackburn, R. M. *Social Stratification and Occupations*, Macmillan, London and Basingstoke.

Wilson, E. (1980), *Only Halfway to Paradise: Women in Postwar Britain 1945–1968*, Tavistock, London.

7 Margaret L. Hedstrom

Beyond feminisation:
clerical workers in the United States from the 1920s through the 1960s

Recent research has advanced our understanding of the nature and significance of clerical work for women in the United States. Historians have analysed the movement of women into office work between 1870 and 1930 and explored the complex process of feminisation, while sociologists and economists have examined the current work experiences and class location of office workers. Research on clerical work has also benefited from a healthy cross-fertilisation between historical and contemporary studies. Sociologists have often borrowed historical interpretations to explain the origins of the feminisation and routinisation of clerical work, while historians have been guided by contemporary issues in framing questions for their research.

In spite of this sharing of questions and concerns, the concentration of historical research on the period before 1930 and the paucity of sociological research prior to the 1970s creates a gap in our understanding of clerical work. Rather than viewing feminisation as a very gradual process which has progressed at different rates under different historical conditions, we tend to consider clerical work 'feminised' once women accounted for the majority of office workers. This approach impedes the development of a long-term view of the changing nature of office work and overlooks several significant changes in the composition of the office workforce.

To develop a historical perspective on changes in office work which extends beyond the movement of women into clerical jobs, it will be necessary to discuss changes in office work in the United States in three periods which deviate somewhat from those traditionally used by historians. The first period, from the 1870s to 1919, was one of initial feminisation of clerical jobs. During this period, women entered the rapidly expanding office work sector primarily by capturing the new fields of stenography and typing. By 1920, women made up almost half of the American clerical workforce and they held more than ninety per cent of all typing and stenographic jobs. The second period, from roughly 1920 to 1940, differs in several important respects from the period of initial feminisation. During the inter-war period, the rate of expansion of the clerical sector slowed considerably and the gender composition of the clerical workforce reached relative stability compared to either the period ending with the First World War or beginning with the Second World War. Feminisation accelerated again between the beginning of the Second World War and 1970 when women's share of clerical jobs increased from one-half to nearly three-quarters. As feminisation proceeded in the post-war period, clerical workers were drawn from a broad spectrum of the female population which included large numbers of older and married women.

Figure 7.1 *Number of clerical workers in the United States, 1870–1970*

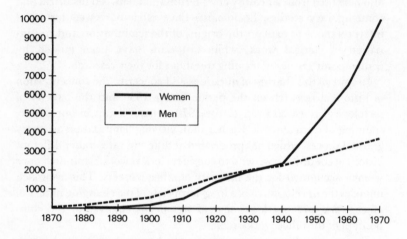

Sources: A. Edwards, *Comparative Occupational Statistics for the United States, 1870 to 1940*; Part of the Sixteenth Census of the Population, US Government Printing Office, Washington, DC, 1943; US Women's Bureau, *Changes in Women's Occupations, 1940–1950*, US Government Printing Office, Washington, DC, 1954, p. 85; US Bureau of the Census, *Occupational Characteristics*, Part of the Eighteenth Census of the Population, Washington, DC, US Government Printing Office, 1963, Table 1; and US Bureau of the Census, *Detailed Characteristics*, Part of the Nineteenth Census of the United States, 1973, Table 226.

This essay also explores some of the obstacles that managers encountered in their efforts to reduce the costs of office work by substituting lower paid women for men, by proposing more efficient work methods, and by introducing new technology. At times, social pressure to provide employment to men and a desire to reduce direct competition between men and women for office jobs limited managers' ability to pursue feminisation. Managers also disagreed over both the importance of curbing office costs and the best methods to do so.

Although feminisation and rationalisation have worked together to enhance managerial control in the office, tensions between gender-based strategies of control and formal, rational work methods have retarded the emergence of a single, coherent approach to office management. Even in the post-war period, managers continued to rely on the attitudes and expectations that women brought with them to the work place as essential elements of managerial control in office work.

The feminisation of typing and stenography, 1870–1919

With few exceptions, historians of the feminisation of clerical work have chosen the period from 1870 to 1930 as the time frame for their studies.[1] During this period of phenomenal growth in the clerical sector, the importance of women to the expansion of clerical work became firmly established. Whereas women accounted for only 2 per cent of all American clerical workers in 1870, by 1930 women made up nearly half of the clerical workforce. The shifting sex composition of the clerical workforce makes office work an interesting occupation for students of gender divisions in work and lends special importance to the period of initial feminisation. Margery Davies views this time frame as the period when both the basic structure of office work and the gender composition of the clerical workforce were established. According to Davies, by 1930 the autonomous male clerks of the 1870s had been replaced by female 'office operatives' or transformed into members of the working class.[2]

The emergence of the corporate form of organisation during the latter half of the nineteenth century greatly increased the demand for salaried managers to plan and co-ordinate the activities of large firms and for clerical workers to handle their numerous transactions. In the United States, the number of clerical workers increased nearly ten-fold between 1870 and the turn of the century, more than doubled in the next decade, and nearly doubled again between 1910 and 1920. The rapid rise in demand for clerical workers, however, does not explain why women as well as men found increasing employment opportunities in clerical jobs during the late nineteenth century.

A complex combination of factors made women attractive as office workers and attracted women to this new and unusual field of work. Employers readily recognised that women accepted office jobs at lower salaries than men. In 1869, seven years after the first experiment with female clerks began at the US Treasury Office, Francis Elias Spinner, the US Treasurer General, concluded that '[s]ome of the female clerks [were] doing more and better work for $900 per annum than many male clerks who were paid double that amount'.[3] According to one recent study of feminisation, the practice of paying women less than men prevailed by the 1880s. Although women's wages for office work were lower than men's, women earned more as clerical workers than in most other acceptable forms of female employment.[4]

The higher educational attainment of women endowed more women than men with basic literacy – one of the requirements for entry into a clerical job. Between 1870 and 1920, women constituted a majority and an increasing percentage of all high school graduates. Women's share of enrolments in private business and commercial courses also rose steadily, increasing from 4 per cent in 1871 to around 60 per cent by 1920. Although the levels of educational achievement among men also rose during this period, there simply were not enough literate men to fill the demand for office workers.[5] In essence, employers faced a choice between hiring less educated men or opening some office jobs to women.

The invention of the typewriter and its gradual introduction into the office was another key factor that facilitated the movement of women into clerical work. Davies contends that there was no apparent evidence of competition between men and women for typist jobs because typewriting never was sex-typed as a man's job. Lisa Fine has suggested that the typewriter was defined as a woman's machine almost from the start. Typewriter companies and their salesmen deliberately chose women to demonstrate the new machine, believing that women's skill at piano playing made them especially effective demonstrators. Although some male stenographers and some employers ridiculed the first generation of women typists and resisted their movement into the office, women rapidly gained a monopoly over typing and its sister occupation of stenography. By the early twentieth century, young men were rejecting stenography as an effeminate occupation, and by 1920 women held 90 per cent of typing and stenographic jobs.[6]

Historians have approached the initial feminisation of office work from two opposite directions, reading quite different conclusions about its implications for women workers at the turn of the century. Some analysts have compared the work experiences and status of the first female clerical workers with those of their male predecessors and concluded that women were able to enter office work only as clerical jobs became rationalised, deskilled, and degraded. Women did not encounter the mobility that early and mid-nineteenth century clerks had from apprentice-like positions as office boys, clerks, and copyists to stable and respectable posts as book-keepers, chief clerks, or perhaps managers of a firm. Rather, office work assumed the characteristics attributed to other jobs that are sex-typed as women's work: relatively low pay, little responsibility, and limited opportunity for advancement.[7]

Some recent studies have reassessed the feminisation of clerical work in the context of the employment opportunities generally available to women in the late nineteenth century and concluded that office jobs offered women a relatively well-paid and high status occupation. Compared to most other working women (with the possible exception of teachers) clerical workers earned more money, commanded greater respect, and achieved more economic and social independence. For the daughters of middle-class parents, clerical work provided a respectable role outside of the home, while for the daughters of working-class parents, office work offered considerable upward mobility. As Fine explains, '[s]een from this perspective, women were drawn to clerical jobs, not relegated to them'.[8]

This interpretation also acknowledges that the women who entered office work were historical agents who played an active role in winning a place for themselves in the office and in changing the prevailing norms of women's role in society. Unlike most other women, who performed domestic labour in the home or worked in physically segregated factories and sweatshops, clerical workers entered the masculine world of business and shared their work places with men. Clerical work provided many young women with a freer space between adolescence and marriage to experiment with and ultimately reshape the role of the modern woman. Many historians have observed the rapid transition from the proper Victorian woman of the late nineteenth century to the independent woman of the 1920s, but only recent studies have revealed the importance of office workers in redefining acceptable roles for young women.[9]

Viewing office work as an expanded employment opportunity for women, and one which women pursued actively, also helps to explain the nature of the broader social debate over women's work in offices. In spite of ample evidence that women accepted office positions at lower pay than men, the issue of competition between women and men for office jobs was secondary to a much deeper concern over the threat that working women posed to traditional views of womanhood. With few exceptions, supporters and opponents of women clerical workers agreed that women's primary role was as wife and mother, but they disagreed over how office work might contribute to or undermine that role. Some opponents questioned whether women had either the physical stamina or moral fortitude to avoid the exhaustion, debilitation, and moral deprevation that might result from their exposure to the competitive, male-dominated world of business, while others believed that women clerical workers would take on mannish traits and shun their domestic responsibilities. Supporters insisted that office work was a healthy experience for young women because they learned thrift, discipline, and self-reliance which prepared them to be better wives and mothers.[10]

The exemplary behaviour of the women who entered clerical work as stenographers and typists between 1870 and the First World War helped to dispel the fears of their most ardent detractors. Most young women dutifully left office work when the opportunity for marriage arrived. Although the first generation of women office workers expanded the definition of appropriate occupations for young women, they did not challenge the centrality of women's domestic role. Moreover, few clerical workers questioned the gender division of labour or the double wage standard for office work.

The period of initial feminisation was vital for establishing the legitimacy of women's presence in the office and for defining the terms of women's employment in clerical jobs. What set women apart from men was not only that they performed different tasks, but that office work had a different meaning in women's lives. As long as women accepted domesticity and motherhood as their primary role, they were welcome in the office as temporary workers who would not compete with men for lifelong careers or opportunities for advancement. This implicit assumption was fundamental in gaining acceptance of women in the office, in structuring women's jobs, and in determining the methods that office managers chose to maintain discipline and control in the office.

The limits of feminisation

Many analyses of feminisation stress the economic advantages to employers of hiring women rather than men in office jobs. It is important to recognise, however, that employers encountered a variety of constraints on their ability to pursue feminisation as a strategy to lower labour costs. Both the unique characteristics of certain office occupations and specific historical conditions affected the timing and the process of changing the gender labels of office jobs. In order to explore certain limitations on the movement of women into office work, it is useful to examine the feminisation of book-keeping and clerk positions and to extend this analysis into the interwar period.

Women began working as book-keepers and clerks in the 1870s, but their movement into these occupations was gradual until the early twentieth century. In 1910, when women had captued more than 80 per cent of typing and stenographic jobs, they held less than 40 per cent of book-keeping and accounting positions and they made up only one fifth of all clerks. The majority of book-keepers and accountants were men until 1930, and they continued to dominate clerk positions until the Second World War. Although employers had ample economic incentives to replace male clerks and book-keepers with women, the apparent competition between men and women for these positions and the slower rate of growth of clerical employment during the interwar period limited their ability to do so.

Changes in business communications which accompanied the creation of national markets in the latter half of the nineteenth century stimulated the expansion of stenography and typing into major office occupations. Many forms of communication which had been handled orally were supplanted by written and typed correspondence, and women were brought into the office as stenographers and typists to accomplish work which had not been done in the past. Jobs for typists and stenographers increased at a much more rapid pace than any other type of office employment in the late nineteenth century. Whereas typists and stenographers accounted for only 3 per cent of the office workforce in 1880, by 1900 they were 15 per cent of all office workers.

Unlike stenographers and typists who filled the demand for a new type of office work, women book-keepers and clerks entered occupations which traditionally had been defined as men's work. The potential for women to displace men or to degrade these occupations by accepting jobs at lower salaries represented an especially potent threat to male hand book-keepers who still retained considerable control over the accounts of many firms. Moreover, women began to enter book-keeping and clerk positions at a time when many firms were experimenting with new methods to cut accounting costs – by subdividing book-keeping work into narrow and specialised tasks and by introducing a variety of new office machines.

A revolution in business accounting practices during the early decades of the twentieth century placed considerable pressure on firms to develop economical and efficient methods for keeping track of complex business transactions. By the turn of the century, the desire among modern managers for greater internal control over production and finances increased the volume and complexity of business accounting and record keeping. During the first half of the twentieth century many firms developed elaborate cost accounting systems to monitor and control inventories, production, sales, and prices. Pressure from the public for greater corporate accountability also added new administrative expenses to the cost of running a business. Progressive Era investigations of railroads, life insurance companies, public utilities, municipal governments, and banks ushered in a wave of reforms in accounting practices which were essential for compliance with new government regulations. In the 1930s, businesses and the government further scrutinised accounting methods as managers and regulators searched for causes of the economic crisis and installed new mechanisms to prevent a recurrence.[11]

Firms could not keep up with the demand for new and more detailed accounting information without greatly expanding their staffs of book-keepers, accountants and clerks. By the turn of the century, women stenographers and typists had already paved the way for the recruitment of women into office work and, therefore, it is not surprising that employers also turned to women to fill new jobs as book-keepers and clerks. Between 1900 and the First World War, women entered clerk and book-keeping positions in increasing numbers, but the departure of men from the labour force during the First World War provided a special impetus to the feminisation of these positions. According to Sharon Strom, managers used both the general shortage of labour in the 1910s and the availability of a variety of new book-keeping and billing machines to replace male hand book-keepers with female machine operators.[12] Bankers, for example, took advantage of the withdrawal of men during the war to speed up the mechanisation of book-keeping. According to one observer, 'the end of the war found women entrenched as bookkeeping-machine operators on customer accounts and other applications of listing and balancing'.[13]

The apparent competition between women and men for book-keeping jobs, however, limited managers' ability to freely replace male hand book-keepers with women. Feminisation, mechanisation, and the subdivision of book-keeping into narrow and discrete tasks threatened the status of the traditional book-keeper and undermined the morale of men who did accounting work. Strom has argued that managers were able to introduce women into book-keeping work only by creating a new hierarchy among book-keepers as women entered this field. The most routine aspects of book-keeping work, such as posting, tallying, and producing bills, were split off from book-keeping and reclassified as women's clerical or machine operating positions. At the same time, the analytical aspects of book-keeping were elevated to the new profession of accounting which was rapidly dominated by men. According to Strom, this process lowered the unit costs of maintaining accounts, obscured the erosion of the book-keeper's position, and reduced the apparent competition between men and women for book-keeping and accounting jobs.[14]

Specific historical conditions also shaped the feminisation of book-keeping and clerk positions. After the First World War, the expansion of clerical work slowed considerably and the movement of women into book-keeping and clerical positions came to a standstill before the gender labels of these occupations were clearly defined. Compared to the 1910s, when the number of office workers increased by more than 80 per cent, the clerical workforce grew by less than 30 per cent in the 1920s and by less than 15 per cent in the 1930s. As the rate of growth in office jobs slowed during the inter-war period, managers were less able to pursue feminisation without making competition between women and men obvious.

Office managers also encountered intense social pressure to keep jobs available for men in the 1930s when high unemployment re-ignited the debate over the propriety of women's employment generally. Some critics of working women held them accountable for the Depression and suggested that their departure from the labour force would eliminate unemployment among men. However, women in sex-typed occupations, such as stenography and typing, were protected to a large extent from pressure to leave the workforce. Even if employers had been inclined to offer typing and stenographic jobs to men, this gesture would have been impractical and costly because few men possessed the skills needed to fill these jobs and men exacted higher salaries than women. [15]

This was not the case with book-keeping and clerk positions. Under the cost-cutting pressures of the Depression, managers had a clear incentive to replace men with lower-paid women, and some did use this opportunity to fire older, male hand book-keepers and to hire younger, cheaper women to replace them.[16] Overall, however, women made no inroads into book-keeping or clerk positions in the 1930s because social pressure to provide jobs to men curbed managers' willingness to further feminise the office workforce. The economic crisis also exposed just how important women's departure from office work upon marriage was to their acceptance as office workers. Grace Coyle observed even before the Depression began that married women were not welcome in clerical jobs:

Employers and employment managers look with suspicion upon married women, although the basis for this attitude rests less upon a scientific study of the relative efficiency of married and unmarried women than a commendable desire to defend the 'American home' from subversive tendencies. Unmarried women regard them as unfair competition who should leave the field to the girl who has no other support.[17]

These attitudes, however, did not discourage married women from seeking office jobs. As Coyle noted, even though clerical work was dominated by single women, the percentage of married women in clerical work doubled during the 1920s.

Pressure for married women to leave the workforce during the Depression did not reverse this trend in the 1930s. More married women sought clerical jobs to help support families and women with clerical jobs were reluctant to give up their jobs when they married. When married women stopped leaving office work as a matter of course, many banks, insurance companies, government agencies, and other major clerical employers erected formal bars against married women's employment. These policies were only partially successful at keeping married women out of offices, but they allowed some firms to demonstrate that they were not denying jobs to men and single women while married women remained on the payroll.[18]

Internal recruitment and promotional policies in most large firms also retarded the entrance of women into jobs as clerks and book-keepers during the inter-war period. As many studies of clerical work have pointed out, the chances that a young man would rise from an office boy to a manager were miniscule by the early twentieth century. Yet this observation should not imply that internal recruitment and promotion became irrelevant. Most firms clung tenaciously to the practice of recruiting all supervisors, department heads, and managers from the ranks of the clerks, and this practice required an ample pool of young men from which to select the most stable and loyal employees for promotions. Moreover, opportunities for advancement were vital to managerial strategies for maintaining the morale of male office workers and building their loyalty to a firm. Because employers were actuely aware that young men entered a firm with only limited possibilities for advancement, they redoubled their efforts to maintain some modest promotional opportunities into senior clerk and book-keeping posts.

Labour shortages during the Second World War again opened new clerical jobs to women and accelerated the feminisation of book-keeping. As men left office work for the war, managers opened routine clerical jobs and more responsible positions as hand book-keepers, auditors, and supervisors to women. The replacement of men with women clerks made the gender division of labour more uniform across firms. The editors of one business magazine commenting on the successful substitution of women for men in jobs as addressograph operators, mimeograph operators, meter clerks and testers, and ledger clerks at a public utility, noted that 'there is great variation in the policies of different companies as to which jobs are traditionally for men and which for women'.[19] By the end of the war, however, women had laid permanent claim to the majority of jobs as book-keepers and clerks. Unlike industrial work, where most women were expected to leave non-traditional jobs in order to make room for returning veterans, few men reclaimed their posts in offices as book-keepers, clerks, or office boys at the end of the war.[20]

The feminisation of routine clerk positions during the war resolved some of the tensions that employers had faced in the 1920s and 1930s between their desire to offer employment opportunities and some upward mobility to young men, and the increasingly limited oppor-tunities for advancement in clerical jobs. Because it was difficult to promise mobility to men and to satisfy them with elementary office positions, firms limited the number of young men hired during the war and transferred women to routine work traditionally done by men. As a manager of the Central Life Insurance Company in Cincinnati explained: 'We think that we should not recruit more young men, or boys, into our organization than for whom we can reasonably expect to have fairly good futures. Marriage will give us better turnover among women and women do not as a rule, expect to go as high as men'.[21]

Many firms also restructured their internal job ladders during the war and stopped the traditional practice of recruiting all managers internally. As one office manager predicted, returning servicemen would not want to return to 'sedentary and unspectacular' desk jobs.[22] With the phenomenal growth in college education after the war, young men stopped joining the office workforce as office boys or clerks and instead entered the world of business as junior exectives with business degrees in hand and formal training in modern management methods. Education had replaced experience as the basic criterion for success in business and the line between men's work and women's work was firmly established.

The feminisation of office work was far more complex than a simple reflection of a capitalist drive to lower labour costs by replacing expensive male workers with cheaper women. As differences between feminisation of typing and stenography and the movement of women into book-keeping and clerk positions suggest, feminisation proceeded rapidly when firms were able to offer men ample employment opportunities and prospects for some upward mobility. Managers were constrained by broader social and cultural values which challenged the propriety of women's employment and questioned the displacement of male breadwinners by women. Managers' concerns over the morale of male workers and their need for a pool of recruits for managerial jobs also retarded the feminisation of jobs which traditionally were filled by men.

Gender and managerial control in office work

The gender division of labour in office work has implications which extend beyond the question of whether men or women fill particular office jobs. In the early decades of the twentieth century, office managers also experimented with new ways to organise the clerical labour process and to increase the productivity of clerical workers. Managers' assumptions about appropriately gendered behaviour among men and women influenced the methods that they chose to increase discipline in offices and perpetuated the use of deeply personal forms of control. Efforts to extend managerial hegemony over office work were also complicated by disagreement among managers over the importance of curbing office costs and the most appropriate methods to do so.

Recent research on the labour process reminds us that managers use a wide variety of methods to increase their control over workers. Managerial techniques to elicit co-operation range from overt measures such as harsh discipline and punitive sanctions against workers who behave inappropriately to less conspicuous efforts at gaining consent from workers for their participation in a labour process that they do not control. Richard Edwards grouped these methods into three broad categories: simple control which relies on close supervision and direct disciplinary sanctions, technical control where control mechanisms are embedded in the organisation and technology of production, and bureaucratic control where managerial authority is institutionalised through formal policies and procedures which define and enforce acceptable behaviour on the job. Although these forms of control are not mutually exclusive, Edwards argues that technical and bureaucratic forms of control have largely replaced simple forms of control.[23]

Most studies of managerial control have examined industrial work performed by men, while most research on managerial control in offices has been focused on the introduction of scientific management in the 1910s and 1920s as the primary technique that office managers used to increase their control over clerical workers. Braverman considered the introduction of scientific management in offices as part of a much broader capitalist drive to deskill workers and increase managerial hegemony in the work place. Davies added a gender dimension to this argument. Although she was more cautious than Braverman about the extent and significance of the scientific office management movement, she also viewed it as vital to both the deskilling and feminisation of office work in the early twentieth century.[24] Scientific office managers made important theoretical contributions to managerial efforts to extend the logic of capitalist relations from the factory into the office, yet it is also important to recognise that they encountered numerous impediments to the widespread adoption of their methods.

It is difficult to determine how many offices adopted scientific management methods because scientific office managers advocated a wide range of reforms from desks and chairs that conformed to the shape of the human body, to new office supplies and filing equipment, to a fundamental restructuring of payment and reward systems.[25] There are indications, however, that some of the recent literature has overestimated the influence of this movement, especially in its most extreme form of measured output and piece rate payment schemes. Office managers publicised their experiments with piece rates widely, but these programs were novelties rather than the norm. For example, a piece work system for dictation machine operators that was installed at the Aetna Life Insurance Company in 1926 attracted considerable attention in the management literature, yet only a handful of insurance companies established work measurement programmes before the mid-1950s.[26]

Scientific office managers have been credited with refining the division of labour and bringing factory methods into the office. With the increasing size of office staffs and the proliferation of detail clerks at their bottom rung, office efficiency experts believed that office work had lost the basic characteristics which distinguished it from mass production. Scientific office management was based on the premise that office workers produced discernable products, such as typed letters, bills, or ledger entries that differed only superficially from other types of commodities. Therefore, the techniques that efficiency engineers used in industry to identify the 'one best way' to perform a job, to eliminate wasted motions, and to tie workers to a fixed routine, could also be used to redesign the office along the lines of the modern factory.

Scientific managers did not invent the division of labour in offices. By the early twentieth century, a complex division of labour was already in place, especially in large firms. The segregation of jobs by sex was most apparent with the feminisation of stenography and typing and some differentiation between the work of men and women in book-keeping, accounting, and clerk positions. Large firms were also divided along functional lines into numerous departments. Some large insurance companies, for example, had more than 200 separate departments all with their own specialised typists, book-keepers and clerks. This functional division of labour kept work groups quite small, facilitated close supervision, and buttressed the power of individual department heads. In many firms, department managers designed work methods, controlled hiring, and set their own standards for discipline and for the pace of work.[27]

Scientific managers hoped to replace idiosyncratic work methods and widely varying expectations for productivity and discipline with a more technically correct division of labour and more uniform standards for measuring performance. As William Henry Leffingwell, the best known advocate of scientific office management explained, 'unless there is an agreement to the contrary, the average worker sells his time and not a definite amount of labor'.[28] Scientific managers encouraged businessmen to consolidate correspondence, filing, book-keeping, and accounting work in centralised service departments, not only to facilitate a smooth flow of work but also to prevent clerks from catering to the petty inconsistencies and peculiarities of minor department managers.[29] Scientific managers, however, were unable to gain enough support from top executives to build a company-wide domain. Even Leffingwell lamented the fact that many top executives viewed office costs as an uncontrollable administrative expense and that they were disinclined to pay attention to the cost of office work as long as their companies showed a profit.[30]

Department heads likewise were reluctant to relinquish their control over office workers or to install piecework systems because they recognised the advantages of maintaining distinctions between office workers and factory workers. During the inter-war period many firms required office workers to keep their salaries secret, and pay increases were matters of individual barter with supervisors. Length of service, ability, attendance, punctuality, and conduct all were considered when pay increases or promotions were granted.[31] This traditional salary structure was an effective way of building company loyalty and securing cooperation from workers. As one office manager explained, 'There is no question but that a salary basis of compensation tends to develop in the average office worker a tendency to think of his position in a far different light from the hourly man.'[32] The salary structure was especially important for motivating men who were expected to remain with a firm for an extended period of time, but women were also aware of its symbolic significance. In her 1929 study of women clerical workers, Coyle noted that they had 'positions', not jobs, and were paid 'salaries', not wages.[33]

Proposals by scientific office managers to pay office workers by the piece for their actual production undermined the traditional salary structure and challenged a well-established gender division of labour. Under the traditional salary system, managers used salary increases to reward workers for proper attitudes and to reproduce appropriately gendered behaviour in the workplace. Men were likely to be rewarded for showing initiative whereas women were discouraged from acting aggressively. As more women entered the clerical work force gender-based strategies of control became increasingly important. M. Christine Anderson argues that many managers considered harsh and formal scientific management methods to be costly and unnecessary because informal mechanisms and an ideology which placed women's primary role in the home were sufficient to control an increasingly feminised work force.[34]

Scientific office managers directed most of their attention toward defining the correct technical division of labour, filling volumes of manuals and textbooks with detailed instructions on how to subdivide office work into narrow tasks and then select the right worker for each specific office job. Because they believed that their methods could be applied to men's and women's jobs alike, the gender division of labour was secondary to their concern with developing the correct methods and organisation of office work. Scientific office managers always referred to typists and 'she' and managers as 'he', but they were more equivocal in the gendered terms that they applied to clerks and most other clerical workers.[35] It is possible that they took the gender division of labour as a given and, therefore, perceived no need to elaborate on this issue. Yet given the lingering confusion over the gender labels of many clerical jobs and the tendency of scientific managers to discuss every other aspect of office work in explicit detail, it seems more likely that they considered a division of labour based solely on gender to be contrary at times to the efficient organisation of office work.

In the post-war period, managers have institutionalised discipline with the extensive use of bureaucratic forms of control in most types of office work. The establishment of written position descriptions, job classification schemes, and clear promotional tracks made many implicit bureaucratic practices part of the formal structure of modern firms. The introduction of computers and the widespread use of systems analysis to redesign and automate routine clerical jobs also extended technical forms of control over many women office workers. Tight schedules, work measurement, and a smooth and continuous flow of work dictated by the demands of automated production routines, increased markedly in the 1950s and 1960s with the automation of office work in large paperwork establishments such as banks and insurance companies.[36]

Nevertheless, managerial control in offices does not conform neatly to either the bureaucratic or technical control models because gender-based strategies of control continue to hold considerable sway in shaping social relations. Even with the creation of separate career tracks for men and women, certain elements of bureaucratic control have only limited applicability to women's clerical jobs. As Edwards explained, managers' ability to obtain workers' tacit acceptance of company rules and policies in exchange for promises of a lifelong career is a key element of bureaucratic control.[37] Such promises, however, have limited pursuasiveness for many women whose departure from the labour force for childbearing and childrearing interrupts their steady progression in a career ladder. Thus office managers continue to depend the attitudes and expectations that women bring with them to the workplace as essential elements of managerial control.

The changing composition of the female clerical force, 1940–1970

In 1940, clerical work was a distinctly young, single women's occupation. Nearly two-thirds of women office workers were single, compared to 44 per cent of women in non-clerical occupations. Clerical workers were also the youngest group of women workers. Their median age of a little over twenty-seven years was five years below the median age of all working women.[38] Between 1940 and 1970, as clerical work became increasing sex-segregated and as women's share of clerical jobs grew from one-half to 75 per cent, the female clerical work force also became more heterogeneous in terms of age and marital status. Shortages of young, single women for clerical jobs encouraged employers to draw on a large, untapped reserve of housewives to fill the expanding number of clerical jobs. Yet changes in the composition of the clerical work force were more complex than the interaction of supply and demand factors would imply.

Theories of labour market segmentation and studies of the sex-typing of occupations help to explain how employers make broad comparisons of the suitability of women and men for specific occupations.[39] In office work, women's alleged deftness at manipulating the typewriter keyboard, their tolerance for routine work, and their willingness to accept subordinate positions have been identified as special female attributes which made women preferable for clerical jobs. Recognising these ascriptive characteristics is essential for understanding the sex segregation of office work. In the post-war period, however, segmentation became more sophisticated. As more married women sought office jobs, employers also used age and marital status to judge the acceptability of women for clerical work.

In spite of persistent labour shortages which started during the Second World War, employers only acquiesced gradually to the employment of older and married women. During the Second World War most firms dropped marriage bars and employed women over age thirty-five in clerical jobs for the first time. Although only a few firms re-established restrictions against the employment of married women after the war, many reinstated formal maximum hiring ages or reverted to informal preferences for young women. A March 1946 survey of employment agencies in New York City concluded that the job prospects for women over age forty were 'returning to their pre-war gloom' because employers wanted attractiveness and glamour rather than experience.[40]

The post-war economic boom introduced a new type of labour crisis in offices. By the late 1940s, large paperwork establishments depended on a steady supply of young, female high school graduates to fill routine clerical jobs. The departure of young women from the labour market after a few years to marry and raise a family was an essential element of clerical employment practices, and hiring cycles even assumed a natural rhythm. As June brides exited, Spring high school graduates stepped in to replace them. This pattern began to unravel as changing demographics and new social and cultural practices reduced the supply of recruits for entry level clerical jobs. Because of low birth rates during the Depression, the number of women in the prime age group for clerical work declined precipitously, while a sharp drop in the age of marriage and the increased enrolment of women in post-secondary education removed potential job applicants from the labour market. By the early 1950s, some large firms were unable to recruit an adequate supply of young women to fill vacancies for clerical jobs.[41]

The number of married women in clerical work increased rapidly in the 1940s, yet life cycle changes continued to shape the composition of the clerical workforce. By the 1950s, when it was a common practice for newlyweds to remain at work until they were pregnant with their first child, the baby shower replaced the bridal shower as the parting ritual for women leaving the office workforce. Although most women with young children withdrew from the paid labour force voluntarily, policies in many offices which required pregnant women to resign coupled with discrimination against older women perpetuated the concentration of young women in clerical jobs. Women in their mid-thirties, who had left clerical work to bear and raise children, often found re-entry into clerical work difficult.[42]

Economic and social considerations contributed to employers' reluctance to open clerical jobs to older women and working mothers. By restricting clerical jobs to young women, employers avoided long-term pension obligations, higher aggregate wage bills which would result from regular salary increases for tenured employees, and potential demands for promotions. In the 1950s, a broad social debate over the proper role of working wives and mothers also retarded their acceptance in the office. Many employers shared a widely-held sentiment that full-time work for women was incompatible with extensive domestic responsibilities. If working mothers were also fulfilling their domestic role, many employers believed that they could not devote their full attention to an office job.[43]

Many managers also believed that young women's attractive physical appearance and submissive personalities made them especially suited for clerical work. Because they did not enter the labour force with preconceived ideas of how the work ought to be performed, young women were presumed to be more willing to accept company policies and procedures and more easily socialised into the behavioural norms of a particular office. Just as employers ascribed certain virtues to younger women, older women were depicted as authoritarian and set in their ways. This characterisation obscured the fact that older women gained some authority by virtue of their age and years of experience which set them apart from the typical young, single clerical worker. Some personnel experts maintained that older women were more critical of management, especially if their supervisors were younger men, while some young managers felt uncomfortable giving orders to older women. As one young executive explained, having an older secretary 'would be like asking my mother to do something. I was brought up to be polite . . . deferential . . . to older women. It's not always possible with a secretary'.[44]

Changing attitudes among young women exposed the limitations of restrictive employment practices and forced employers to reassess the virtues and liabilities of women with different social and demographic characteristics. In the 1950s and early 1960s, young women took advantage of the tight labour market to shop around for the best job and to demand higher pay and liberal benefits. This behaviour placed pressure on firms to keep salaries, benefits, and working conditions competitive in order to attract and retain young workers. Once on the job, managers found that young women were less submissive than they had been in the past. These new attitudes were reflected in higher absenteeism and turnover, lateness, frequent use of the telephone for personal calls, long coffee breaks, and a lack of pride in work. Moreover, by the late 1950s, many employers were convinced that young applicants' grammar, spelling, typing, shorthand and office practice skills did not meet basic standards which had been in place since the 1930s.[45]

Faced with a choice between hiring younger women who lacked adequate skills and proper attitudes or compromising on age preferences, clerical employers gradually became more receptive toward older women. Some firms found that older women were more stable and dependable because they were raised in an era of stricter discipline or needed a steady income to help support their families. The social and emotional skills of the housewife also became defined as assets that would help her to adapt to the demands of office work. Unlike earlier characterisations of older women as rigid and inflexible, the housewife returning to office work was portrayed as especially able to sublimate her own desires to the demands of the organisation because of her years of experience in putting the needs of her family before her own.[46]

Lingering discrimination against older women in office work and social concern over the propriety of paid employment by wives and mothers shaped the terms of their integration into the clerical work force. Working wives and mothers were under considerable pressure to demonstrate that they were capable of being good office workers, good wives and good mothers all at the same time. In the context of the social values of the 1950s and early 1960s this meant managing home and work responsibilities without demanding special allowances for personal and family needs from employers or neglecting domestic duties at home. As a 1961 article directed at married secretaries stressed, working wives themselves were agents of change. Gaining acceptance of the working wife, whether from a resentful husband or from an employer who was prejudiced against married women, depended on her ability to manage her double role.[47]

There are important similarities between the initial feminisation of clerical jobs in the late nineteenth century and the movement of older and married women into clerical work during the post-war period. First, older and married women were recruited to meet a rapid increase in the demand for clerical workers in the post-war period, just as young single women filled a similar demand in the late nineteenth century. Wives and mothers did not work for lower wages than single women, but their entrance into office work expanded the pool of applicants for clerical jobs and allowed employers to avoid pressure for wage increases in a tight labour market. In the post-war period, employers also abandoned marital status and age restrictions rather than hire younger women who lacked adequate skills and the proper deportment for clerical work. In the late nineteenth century, employers made a similar compromise by hiring women rather than recruiting less educated men.

In both periods, expanded employment opportunities for women who traditionally had remained outside the paid labour force challenged widely held assumptions about women's proper role in the private sphere of home and family. By leaving the labour force to marry and raise children, the first generations of clerical workers demonstrated that their brief exposure to office work would not undermine their primary role as wives and mothers. At the same time, however, they created a respectable new role for young women between adolescence and marriage. In the 1950s and 1960s, working wives and mothers overcame opposition to their employment outside the home only by proving that they could manage both domestic and work responsibilities. Although they accepted much of the double burden for paid and unpaid labour, many working wives and mothers considered office work a favourable alternative to the idleness and isolation of an exclusively domestic role.

The entrance of older and married women into office work during the post-war period signalled a significant shift in the meaning of clerical jobs for women. Older and married women who re-entered the labour force and remained on the job for an extended period of time undermined a well-established pattern of regular turnover of the office work force. Clerical work, which had been a temporary work experience for young women between high school graduation and marriage, became a long-term occupation with increasingly brief interruptions to bear and care for young children. Yet the basic structure of office occupations of narrow and specialised jobs with few opportunities for advancement, growth, or long-term satisfaction remained essentially unchanged.

As recent reassessments of the initial feminisation of clerical work remind us, it is important to evaluate clerical work in the context of a sex segregated labour market. Until the post-war period, older and married women not only were crowded into typical female jobs, they were also largely excluded from office work. Older and married women struggled against discrimination and prejudice to win a place for themselves in the office and to find an alternative to factory or sales jobs. In a period when the gender division of labour remained unquestioned, opening clerical jobs to a more diverse group of women created new employment opportunities for a broad spectrum of the female population. To view this change otherwise is to understate the extent, sophistication, and significance of sex segregation in the workplace.

Notes

1 M. W. Davies, *Woman's Place Is at the Typewriter: Office Work and Office Workers, 1870–1930*, Temple University Press, Philadelphia, 1982; E. J. Rotella, *From Home to Office: U.S. Women at Work, 1870–1930*, UMI Research Press, Ann Arbor, 1981; L. M. Fine, ' "The Record Keepers of Property": the Making of a Female Clerical Labor Force in Chicago, 1870–1930', unpublished PhD thesis, University of Wisconsin, Madison, 1985; and A. J. Rapone, 'Clerical Labor Force Formation: the Office Woman in Albany, 1870–1930', unpublished PhD thesis, New York University, New York, 1981.

2 Davies, *Woman's Place*, p. 5.

3 'Women in business: I', *Fortune*, XII, July 1935, pp. 53–4. The formation of the clerical work force in the US federal government is treated extensively in C. S. Aron, *Ladies and Gentlemen of the Civil Service: Middle Class Workers in Victorian America*, Oxford University Press, New York and Oxford, 1987.

4 I. DeVault, 'Sons and Daughters of Labor: Class and Clerical Work in Pittsburgh, 1870s–1910s', unpublished PhD thesis, Yale University, New Haven, 1985, p. 66.

5 Davies, *Woman's Place*, pp. 56–8; Rotella, *From Home to Office*, pp. 152–7; Fine, 'Record keepers of property', pp. 144–85; Rapone, 'Clerical labor force formation', pp. 90–127; and J. Weiss, 'Educating for clerical work: the nineteenth century private commercial school', *Journal of Social History*, XIV, 1981, pp. 407–23.

6 Davies, *Woman's Place*, pp. 53–5, and Fine, 'Record keepers of property', pp. 91–104. For an examination of an important counter example to feminisation, see A. Baron, 'Contested terrain revisited: the social construction of gender and skill in the printing industry', in B. Wright, *et al.*, (eds.), *Women, Work and Technology*, University of Michigan Press, Ann Arbor, 1987.

7 H. Braverman, *Labor and Monopoly Capital*, Monthly Review Press, New York, 1974, pp. 293–312, and Davies, *Woman's Place*.

8 Fine, 'The record keepers of property', p. 82; Rapone, 'Clerical labor force formation', pp. 181–217; and Devault, 'Sons and daughters of labor', pp. 80–115. For examples of this perspective applied to other typical female occupations, see B. Melosh, '*The Physician's Hand': Work Culture and Conflict in American Nursing*, Temple University Press, Philadelphia, 1982, and S. P. Benson, *Counter Cultures: Saleswomen, Managers and Customers in American Department Stores, 1890–1940*, University of Illinois Press, Urbana, 1986.

9 Aron, *Ladies and Gentlemen*, pp. 162–83, and L. Fine, 'Between two worlds: business women in a Chicago boarding house, 1900–1930', *Journal of Social History*, XIX, 1986, pp. 511–19.

10 Davies, *Woman's Place*, pp. 79–96.

11 S. H. Strom, 'Beyond the typewriter: the feminization of bookkeeping, 1910–1940', unpublished paper presented at the Berkshire Conference on Women's History, Northampton, Mass., May 1984, pp. 2–7.

12 Strom, 'Beyond the typewriter', pp. 8–9.

13 E. Erickson, *The Employment of Women in Offices*, US Women's Bureau, Bulletin No. 120, Washington, DC, 1934, p. 16.

14 Strom, 'Beyond the typewriter', pp. 10–15.

15 A. Kessler-Harris, *Out to Work: a History of Wage-Earning Women in the United States*, Oxford, 1982, pp. 250–72.

16 Strom, 'Beyond the typewriter', p. 15.

17 G. Coyle, 'Women in the clerical occupations', *Annals of the American Academy of Political and Social Science*, CXLIII, May 1929, p. 183.

18 Kessler-Harris, *Out to Work*, pp. 252–7; L. Scharf, *To Work and to Wed: Female Employment, Feminism and the Great Depression*, Greenwood Press, Westport, Conn., 1980; Erickson, *Employment of Women in Offices*, pp. 12–13; H. A. Byrne, *The Age Factor as It Relates to Women in Business and the Professions*, US Women's Bureau, Bulletin No. 117, 1934, pp. 10–11; R. Shallcross, *Should Married Women Work?*, Public Affairs Committee, New York, 1940.

19 'Business tackles the office problem', *American Business*, XII, Sept. 1942, p. 20.

20 For an analysis of the reversal of women's temporary gains in industrial work at the end of the war, see R. Milkman, *Gender at Work: The Dynamics of Job Segregation by Sex during World War II*, University of Illinois Press, Urbana, 1987.

21 R. H. Steubing, 'Selection and development of office personnel in the emergency', *NOMA Forum*, XVII, April, 1942, p. 32.

22 'Office management in the war', *American Business*, XIV, April 1944, p. 46.

23 R. Edwards, *Contested Terrain: The Transformation of the Workplace in the Twentieth Century*, Basic Books, New York, 1979. For other interpretations of managerial control, see Braverman, *Labor and Monopoly Capital*; D. Clawson, *Bureaucracy and the Labor Process*, Monthly Review Press, New York, 1980; and M. Buroway, *Manufacturing Consent*, University of Chicago Press, Chicago, 1979.

24 Braverman, *Labor and Monopoly Capital*, pp. 304–15, and Davies, *Woman's Place*, pp. 97–128.

25 For a discussion of the technological and managerial contributions of scientific office managers, see S. Cohn, *The Process of Occupational Sex-Typing: The Feminization of Clerical Labor in Great Britain*, Temple University Press, Philadelphia, 1986, pp. 81–9.

26 For examples of early piece rate plans in insurance companies, see M. A. Bills, 'An application of principles of the individual bonus plan to home office clerical work', *Proceedings of the 1927 Conference of the Life Office Management Association*, New York, 1927, pp. 155–9; H. L. Rhodes, 'Paying additional compensation for production', *LOMA Conference Proceedings*, 1927, pp. 160–72; and H. C. Pennicke, 'Compensation in accordance with piece rates and production bonuses', *LOMA Conference Proceedings*, 1927, pp. 189–98. According to two surveys of insurance companies conducted in the 1960s, only a few companies installed work measurement programmes before the mid-1950s. See G. L. Wood, 'A survey of cost reduction programs in life insurance companies in the U. S. and Canada', Houston, 1963(?), typescript; and E. C. Headley, 'LOMA work measurement survey results', *Best's Review*, Life edition, LXX, Nov. 1969, pp. 82–7.

27 W. Breiby, 'Organization and routine changes which occur in successive stages in the development of a life company', *Proceedings of the 1931 Conference of the Life Office Management Association*, New York, 1931, pp. 15–51.

28 W. H. Leffingwell, *Scientific Office Management*, A. W. Shaw, Chicago, 1917, p. 41.

29 W. H. Leffingwell, *Office Management: Principles and Practice*, A. W. Shaw, Chicago, 1925, pp. 119–22.

30 Leffingwell, *Office Management*, p. 160. See also F. L. Rowland, 'Extra wage incentives plans for office workers', in American Management Association, *Office Executive Series*, No. 11, 1926, pp. 3–7.

31 US Personnel Classification Board, *Report of the Wage and Personnel Survey*, US Government Printing Office, Washington, DC, 1929, pp. 280–2.

32 G. H. F. Gardner, *Practical Office Supervision*, McGraw-Hill, New York, 1929, p. xii.

33 Coyle, 'Women in the clerical occupations', p. 187.

34 M. C. Anderson, 'Gender, class, and culture: women secretarial and clerical workers in the United States, 1925–1955', unpublished PhD thesis, Ohio State University, Columbus, 1986, pp. 63–5.

35 Davies, *Woman's Place*, pp. 119–20, contends that scientific managers referred to clerks and stenographers as 'she'. In my reading of scientific management literature I found that the pronoun 'she' was reserved almost exclusively for references to stenographers and typists and that scientific office managers used 'he' to refer to office workers generally and to most clerks. Clearly, scientific office managers did not question the sex-typing of typing and stenography as women's work, but when they suggested that managers could use their methods to replace high-priced clerks with cheaper ones, this did not necessarily mean replacing men with women.

36 I. Hoos, *Automation in the Office*, Public Affairs Press, Washington, DC, 1961, pp. 65–72; A. Gray, 'Problems of adjustment in the automated office', *Personnel*, XLI, July/August 1964, pp. 43–8; and 'Effects of mechanization and automation in offices: Part II', *International Labor Review*, March 1960, pp. 266–7.

37 Edwards, *Contested Terrain*, p. 21.

38 US Women's Bureau, *Changes in Women's Occupations, 1940–1950*, Bulletin No. 253, US Government Printing Office, Washington DC, 1954, p. 85.

39 V. K. Oppenheimer, *The Female Labor Force in the United States*, Institute of International Studies, University of California, Berkeley, 1970; Edwards, *Contested Terrain*, pp. 163–77; D. M. Gordon, R. Edwards, and M. Reich, *Segmented work, divided workers*, DC Heath, Lexington, Mass., 1982, pp. 4–17 and 204–6; and A. Kessler-Harris, 'Stratification by sex: understanding the history of working women', M. Stevenson, 'Women's wages and job segregation', and F. D. Blau, 'Sex segregation of workers by enterprise', in *Labor Market Segmentation*, R. Edwards, M. Reich and D. M. Gordon (eds.), D. C. Heath, Lexington, Mass., 1975, Chapters 8–10.

40 J. Klein, 'Survey shows jobs on the wane for older women', *New York Herald Tribune*, 17, March 1946, Section 2, p. 5.

41 'Wanted: 600,000 office workers', *The Management Review*, 1956, pp. 179–80; 'The coming pinch in office personnel', *The Management Review*, 1956, pp. 563–5; and 'Secretaries wanted!', *The Management Review*, 1957, pp. 43–4.

42 US Women's Bureau, *'Older' Women as Office Workers*, Bulletin No. 248, US Government Printing Office, Washington DC, 1953, pp. 38–40; National Manpower Council, *Work in the Lives of Married Women*, Columbia University Press, New York, 1958, pp. 62–5; and 'Age restrictions in hiring practices', *American Business*, XXVII, Sept. 1957, pp. 25–8.

43 D. Quinn, 'Woman's power: what about the married woman employee?', *The Secretary*, XVIII, Jan. 1958, pp. 20–1, and H. A. Rusk, 'Hidden sources of manpower: I', American Management Association, *Office Management Series*, No. 129, New York, 1952, p. 11. For a discussion of the broader debate over working mothers, see L. Y. Weiner, *From Working Girl to Working Mother*, University of North Carolina Press, Chapel Hill, 1985, pp. 112–25.

44 L. McCracken, 'The job outlook', *Today's Secretary*, LXVII, Jan. 1965, p. 19, and W. W. Suojanen, 'Supervising older clerical workers', *Personnel*, XXXIV, May/June 1958, p. 18.

45 Dartnell Corporation, *Personnel Policies and Salary Administration in 200 Offices,* Chicago, 1950, p. 3; 'Here she comes!', *Office Management,* XV, April 1954, p. 11; A. Lewis and E. S. Bobroff, 'What secretarial shortage?', *Personnel,* XXXIX, Sept./Oct. 1962, pp. 55–9; E. S. Stanton, 'Why can't I get a good secretary?', *Personnel Journal,* XLI, Feb. 1962, pp. 64–5; D. Dilworth, 'The job shopper', *Administrative Management,* XXIII, July 1962, pp. 47–50; O. Lipstreu, 'Are today's workers different?' *Office Executive,* XXVIII, May 1953, pp. 34–5; M. French, 'Is it true what they say about secretaries?', *Today's Secretary,* LXV, Sept. 1962, pp. 52–3; S. Dorst, 'The secretarial crisis', *Today's Secretary,* LXV, March 1963, pp. 23–5; and 'Is promptness a vanishing virtue', *Modern Office Procedures,* XIV, Jan. 1969, pp. 20–2.

46 'Wanted: perfect secretary', *Administrative Management,* XVI, Dec. 1965, p. 12, and 'Mrs. secretary: the changing role of the working wife', *Today's Secretary,* LXIX, Oct. 1966, p. 30.

47 J. Martinson, 'Mrs. secretary: the future lies ahead', *Today's Secretary,* LXIII, April 1961, pp. 26–7, 55.

Index